Solve Your Problems
—The Birbal Way

Insights from the legendary guru to solve family, professional and business problems

Anita S.R. Vas
Luis S.R. Vas

D0967286

PUSTAK MAHAL®
Delhi • Bangalore • Mumbai • Patna • Hyderabad

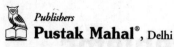

Publishers
Pustak Mahal®, Delhi

J-3/16 , Daryaganj, New Delhi-110002
☎ 23276539, 23272783, 23272784 • *Fax:* 011-23260518
E-mail: info@pustakmahal.com • *Website:* www.pustakmahal.com

Sales Centres

10-B, Netaji Subhash Marg, Daryaganj, New Delhi-110002
☎ 23268292, 23268293, 23279900 • *Fax:* 011-23280567
E-mail: rapidexdelhi@indiatimes.com

Branch Offices

Bangalore: ☎ 22234025
E-mail: pmblr@sancharnet.in • pustak@sancharnet.in
Mumbai: ☎ 22010941
E-mail: rapidex@bom5.vsnl.net.in
Patna: ☎ 3294193 • *Telefax:* 0612-2302719
E-mail: rapidexptn@rediffmail.com
Hyderabad: *Telefax:* 040-24737290
E-mail: pustakmahalhyd@yahoo.co.in

Printed at : Unique Colour Carton, Mayapuri, Delhi-110064

Dedication

For our Godchildren, Heidi, Ulrich and Desiree; and nephews Jose, Filipe, Nigel, Eric and Hansel.

May they grow up to be as clever as Birbal.

Contents

Introduction

Centuries ago the Great Mughal Emperor Humayun died, leaving his kingdom to a 13-year-old prince named Akbar. Bright and bold, the boy fought fierce battles with myriad enemies to defend the vast kingdom that his father had left him. Finally, peace settled across his beautiful domain and Akbar inaugurated a Golden Age in India.

The young king encouraged everyone to worship in their own ways. Subjects of every description and origin stood as equals before him. Akbar loved philosophy and all the fine arts, and sought the company of the wisest and most talented men he could find inside and outside his kingdom, bringing them to the Imperial Court. Nine of these exceptional men were such gifted and rare examples of talent that people called them *Nava Ratna* – 'The Nine Jewels of the Mughal Crown' – since their value exceeded the price of precious stones.

One of them, Tansen, was a singer so skilled that candles were said to burst into flame at the sheer power of his song. Another, Daswant, was a painter who became First Master of the Age. Todar Mal was a financial wizard. Abul Fazl was a great historian, and his brother, Faizi, a noted poet. Abud us-Samad was a brilliant calligrapher and designer of Imperial coins. Man Singh was an exceptional military strategist. Mir Fathullah Shirazi was a man of many parts: financier, philosopher, physician and astronomer. But of all Akbar's Nine Jewels, the people's favourite was his Minister – or Wazir – Birbal, who was noted for his cleverness, generosity and sense of justice.

Birbal became one of the best-loved figures in the folklore of India. For generations, the Birbal stories have delighted children and grown-ups alike across all regions of the country.

Jalaludin Mohammed Akbar Padshah Ghazi, Emperor of India, ruled from 1560 to 1605. Akbar was great in an age of great rulers: Elizabeth I of England, Henry IV of France, Philip II of Spain, Sulaiman the Magnificent of Turkey, and Shah Abbas the Great of Persia.

Akbar was generous and just to all men, but he could be violent and overpowering when called for. His magnetic personality won the love and affection of his people and the respect and admiration of his enemies.

The Emperor excelled at riding, polo and swordsmanship, and he was a brilliant marksman with his musket. He was courageous, often fighting personally in the heat of battle. He was an outstanding general, a master of speed, surprise and logistics. His lightning conquests of India, from the Hindu Kush to Bengal, were feats of military genius.

Akbar worked hard at his duties as a king, sleeping only three hours a night. Although he was illiterate (it has been conjectured that he was probably dyslexic), he had legions of scholars who read to him. His son, Prince Sultan Salim, later the Emperor Jahangir, wrote that no one could have guessed that Akbar was illiterate. He had an insatiable appetite for religion, philosophy, music, architecture, poetry, history and painting. He built an empire that enjoyed long-lasting peace, prosperity and high cultural refinement.

The empire of the Mughals was vast and fabulously rich. Akbar's lower taxes and rising conquests created wealth for the people and mounting treasure for the Crown. European visitors noted that just one province of Akbar's empire, Bengal, was wealthier than France and England combined. But the Emperor's most precious asset was his quick-witted Wazir.

Birbal was born to a poor Brahmin family of Tikawanpur on the banks of the River Jamuna. He rose to the exalted level of minister at Akbar's Court by virtue of his razor-sharp wit. He was an accomplished poet, writing under the pen name

'Brahma', and a collection of his verse is preserved to this day in the Bharatpur Museum.

Birbal's duties at Court were administrative and military, but his close friendship with the Emperor was enhanced by Akbar's love of wisdom and subtle humour. In Birbal – who was 14 years older than Akbar – the young king found a true sympathiser and companion. In an attempt to unify his Hindu and Muslim subjects, when Akbar founded a new religion of universal tolerance, the Din-i-Ilahi, or 'Divine Faith', there was only one Hindu among the handful of his followers, and that was Birbal.

Akbar's Court was mobile, a tradition inherited from his nomadic ancestors, the Mongols of Central Asia. (*Mughal* is Urdu for Mongol.) The Emperor ruled sometimes from the fortress of Agra and sometimes from the elegant city of Lahore. During the period of these tales, 1571 to 1585, Akbar held court in the scintillating city that he had built for himself – Fatehpur Sikri.

Many courtiers were jealous of Birbal's meteoric rise to fortune and power and, according to popular accounts, they were endlessly plotting his downfall.

The poet, however, died with a sword in his hand. This happened in February 1586 while he was leading an expedition to subdue an Afghan tribe in north-western India. Akbar, it is said, was inconsolable when he heard the news.

The character of Akbar in these stories is rather farfetched. But historically, Birbal is hardly talked about. It is not clear how many of the Birbal stories can really be attributed to Birbal. Many of these tales were probably invented by village storytellers over the ages and simply attributed to Birbal and Akbar because their characters seemed appropriate. But there is no doubt that they make entertaining and instructive reading.

We would like to suggest that there is a deeper psychological and sociological reason behind the Birbal stories. They tend to show to the subject people under the Moghuls that although the Emperor is enlightened and virtually all-powerful, his Raja, Birbal, coming from the subject stock, is the cleverer, wiser man, getting the Emperor out of all kinds of difficulties and outwitting him in debate. The tales served to boost the morale of the subjects of the Moghul Empire and their descendants.

The stories also illustrate the leader's sagacity and problem-solving acumen of Birbal or whoever thought them up.

At a time when it is fashionable to identify various management and leadership styles with historical and mythical personalities like Attila the Hun, Winnie the Pooh, Mulla Nasiruddin, Confucius and Jesus Christ, and with philosophical systems and religious books like Zen, Taoism, the Kabballah, the Bible, the Bhagwad Gita and Sufism, we thought it would be appropriate to underscore the managerial wisdom and problem-solving principles which Birbal's stories illustrate.

So, we have retold some of the Birbal stories that we gathered and at the end of each we have pointed out the management moral it teaches, turning Birbal into a virtual Edward de Bono of the 16th century whose wisdom and lateral thinking remain as fresh as ever. We have divided each story into two parts. The first part consists of the problem; the second part provides Birbal's solution.

You are encouraged to pause just before the solution is given and think of your own solution to the problem. Only when you have thought of one or more solutions should you read Birbal's solution. There is no more effective way of honing your own creativity.

You are also encouraged to sharpen your creativity by thinking up additional management ideas that these stories evoke. We shall be happy if you send us more such stories with your own interpretations of the principles they illustrate, to include them in future editions of this book.

At the end of the book we have devised a process which we have termed BIRBAL (an acronym) and which you can use to solve your own problems.

We have written this book jointly to provide you with a balanced perspective of the issues explored in it. We would appreciate your comments.

Luis S.R. Vas & Anita S.R. Vas
E-mail: vasluis@hotmail.com

1. First Meeting

Problem

Emperor Akbar had a mobile court which one day found itself in a village in what is now Madhya Pradesh, where a young Brahmin farmer, Mahesh Das, lived. Mahesh heard a herald announce that Emperor Akbar would award a thousand gold coins to the artist who pleased him with the most realistic portrait of the Emperor.

On the appointed day and time, there was a beeline of artists before the Court; each had a covered picture of the Emperor. Everyone in the Court was anxious to find who would get the coveted prize of one thousand gold coins.

Akbar, sitting on a high-throne, received the folded portraits, and rejected them one by one with his cryptic comments.

"No. This is not exactly what I am now."

The poor Brahmin, Mahesh Das, who later became famous as Birbal, was waiting for his chance. He was the last to show the portrait he carried with him.

Birbal's Solution

When Mahesh's turn came, Emperor Akbar was already piqued: "Are you like the rest of the incapables who have unsatisfactorily produced my portraits, which don't exactly show me what I am now?"

Whereupon Mahesh, without fear yet in a tone of humility, said: "Look, my Emperor, into it and satisfy yourself."

Strangely, it was not a drawing or painting, but a mirror that emerged from the folds of Mahesh's garments to show the Emperor exactly what he was then.

"The best replica of Emperor Akbar," everyone chorused.

Akbar received Mahesh Das with open arms to the applause of everyone in the open Court, and rewarded him with a thousand gold coins. He also gave Mahesh a ring with the Royal Seal and invited him to meet the Emperor in his capital, Fatehpur Sikri.

Management Moral 1: *Learn what your client wants and give it to him so that his need is fulfilled. What Akbar wanted was not an artist's impression of himself, but reality – which only a mirror could provide.*

Management Moral 2: *With all humility, Mahesh made the Emperor realise that it was not possible to get what he wanted. And for this he won the prize, despite not having done what the Emperor wanted – a perfect portrait. An argument with one's superiors would be termed arrogant behaviour and could get one the sack. But practical proof of the impossibility of the Emperor's request made him the wiser for it and earned the contestant his reward! So by all means, communicate what you have in mind frankly, but diplomatically.*

■ ■ ■

2. Mahesh Das
Seeks His Fortune

When Mahesh became a young man, he took the few coins, which were all his savings, along with the ring of the Royal Seal, bade his mother farewell, and set out on the long road to the new capital of the empire, Fatehpur Sikri.

Never, in his childhood, had he seen such a sea of humanity as he found in the splendid capital. Mountains of sweet delicacies, coloured golden, green and red, were sold in the bazaar, along with precious silks, elegant lambs' wool hats and gold jewellery hammered as thin and fine as a feather. Mahesh was wide-eyed with astonishment. He felt as though he could meander through the labyrinthine alleys and extensive thoroughfares for months and discover new delights all the time.

Huge camels ambled past, water-sellers called out with their nasal cries, acrobats and magicians drew curious crowds, incense spiralled from the many temples, and then, as if from nowhere, the haunting notes of a flute would reverberate amidst the milling crowd.

Mahesh had no little trouble keeping his mind upon the purpose of his journey and headed resolutely for the massive, red walls of the palace.

The palace gate was so massive and richly carved, Mahesh thought it was the entrance to the Emperor's own home! But it was far from that. Beautiful as it was, it was merely the outermost edge of the great city within a city, which was the Imperial Court.

As soon as the guard on duty noticed the astonished gaze of this simple-looking country boy, he slashed the air with his spear and barred Mahesh's path.

"Where do you think you're going, oaf?"

"I have come to see the Emperor," said Mahesh, softly.

"Oh, have you? Why, how very fortunate. His Majesty has been wondering when you'd turn up!" he uttered sarcastically.

"Yes, I know. Well, now I'm here."

"Fool! Do you think Shah Akbar has nothing to do but entertain ignorant yokels? Go away!"

Mahesh looked at the quivering moustache of this arrogant warrior and half-smiled.

"Please, brother. When you were younger, no doubt you fought wonderfully on the empire's frontiers. Now that they have given you this easy job, why do you want to risk it?"

The guard's jaw dropped.

"Why you impudent worm! I'll lop your head off with a single... I'll... I'll..."

14

But he stopped short as Mahesh held out Akbar's ring. Even a guard could recognise the Imperial Seal.

"Our good Emperor receives all who come to see him. Many years ago he sent for me. Now let me pass."

Annoyed, the guard saw he would have to admit the young man. But he was unwilling to let him off scot-free.

Problem

"You can pass on one condition," he scowled. "If you obtain anything from the Emperor, you will give half to me."

"Agreed," smiled Mahesh, and went by. Mahesh was determined to teach the guard a lesson. He could not put up with corrupt practices.

Shady trees swayed with the breeze as Mahesh trod his way through the royal gardens. Cooling fountains murmured, and the perfume of roses wafted invisibly through the air.

Each building he passed seemed more magnificent than the last. Finally, he recognised that a pavilion made of shimmering marble, with a forest of columns and fretted arches, must be the Hall of Public Audience. So many richly dressed courtiers thronged there that they all began to look the same to his untutored eyes. His heart pounded as he felt that each person his gaze rested upon might turn out to be the Emperor.

At last he saw a man of simple elegance, seated upon a throne of gold studded with flashing gems, whose nobility glistened through his eyes. He needed to look no further. This was Akbar.

Birbal's Solution

Pushing past the many Uzbek generals, Rajput princes and Persian artists, Mahesh prostrated himself before the throne and caught the Emperor's gaze.

"May your shadow never wane, O Full Moon!"

Akbar smiled.

15

"Ask, O one of the bright prospects."

"Sire," said Mahesh, rising. "I have come at your command, which none dare disobey." And he handed back to the Emperor the ring, which the latter had given the country boy so many years ago.

Akbar laughed with pleasure. "Welcome, welcome. What can I do for you? What can I give you? What is your heart's desire?"

The courtiers hushed at this unusually generous reception by the Emperor. Who was this shabby-looking young man?

Mahesh thought for a moment and then said evenly: "I would like you to punish me with one hundred lashes."

You could have heard a pin drop upon the polished marble floor.

"What!" exploded the Emperor. "A hundred lashes? But you have done nothing wrong!"

"Will Your Majesty go back on his promise to fulfil my heart's desire?"

"Well, no; a King must always keep his word..."

So, with great reluctance and perplexity, Akbar ordered Mahesh's back to be stripped and a hundred lashes of the whip to be laid upon it by the Court executioner. To the acute interest of all the assembled courtiers, Mahesh endured every stroke with a stony expression and without uttering a sound.

But when the whip had cracked for the fiftieth time, he suddenly jumped up and cried: "Stop!"

"Ah!" exclaimed Akbar. "Then you see how foolish you are being."

"No, Sire. It is only that when I came here to see you, I was unable to enter the palace, until I promised the guard at the front gate half of whatever the Emperor's generosity might get me. So I have taken my half of the hundred lashes. Please be kind enough to deliver the rest to him."

The entire crowd screeched with laughter, Akbar the loudest of all. His fingers snapped and in less time than it takes to tell, the unhappy guard was hauled into the Presence Chamber to receive his humiliating "bribe".

When he was dragged out in disgrace, Akbar turned to Mahesh and said: "You are as brave as when you were a young man and, possibly, you have grown cleverer. I have tried in many ways to weed out corruption at my Court, but your little trick today will do more to make greedy officials honest than if I passed a thousand laws. From now on, since you are so wise, you shall be called 'Birbal'. And you shall stay by my side and advise me in all matters."

Management Moral: *Uphold ethical standards as dramatically as you can to win universal approval and admiration. Ethics is the basis of all effective management. Nothing can replace it.*

Besides, the pursuit of justice can be more rewarding than greed or giving in to the lure of quick lucre; it got Birbal a lifetime's prestigious post rather than only a bagful of wealth.

■ ■ ■

3. Birbal's Journey to Paradise

Problem

The Court barber nursed his hatred for Birbal and plotted against him daily. One day he struck upon a plan and so, when Emperor Akbar next called him to trim his beard, he said: "You know, Your Majesty, last night I dreamed about your father."

The Great Mughal at once showed interest. "Tell me what he said to you."

"He is very happy in Paradise, but he says that all the inhabitants of Heaven are terrible bores. He would like you to send him someone who can talk to him and keep him amused."

Of course, no one possessed wit like Birbal's and although Akbar prized him very much, to appease his poor father in Paradise, he would consent to give him up. Naturally, the only way of reaching Heaven is through death.

When Birbal responded to the Emperor's summons, Akbar said: "I think you love me enough, Birbal, to make any sacrifice for my sake."

"You know I do, Your Majesty."

"Then I would like you to go to Heaven and keep my dear father company."

"Very well," Birbal said, "but please give me a few days to prepare."

"Certainly," said the Mughal, delighted. "You are doing me a great favour. I will give you a week."

Birbal's Solution

Birbal went home and dug a deep pit, which would serve as his own grave. But he also excavated a secret tunnel that opened under the floor of his house. Then he returned to the Imperial Court.

"Your Highness," he said, "in accordance with an old family tradition, I would like to be buried near my house – and, if you don't mind, I would like to die by being buried alive. It is easier to get into Heaven that way, you know."

So, to the great happiness of the Court barber, Birbal was buried alive. Of course, he made his way at once through the tunnel into his own house, where he stayed in concealment for over six months.

At the end of that time, with his hair and beard grown long and shaggy, he came out of hiding and obtained an audience with the Great Mughal.

"Birbal!" cried the Emperor. "Where have you come from?"

"From Paradise, Your Majesty. I spent such a lovely time with your father that he gave me special permission to return to earth."

"Did he give you any message for his son?"

"Just one, Your Highness. Do you see my whiskers and long hair? Well, it seems very few barbers make it to Heaven. Your father asks you to send him yours at once."

Management Moral: *Ill will begets ill will and can even lead to a chain reaction. Often you have to be innovative to combat it. Perhaps by using goodwill to beget goodwill, which would probably also result in its own chain reaction.*

■ ■ ■

4. All for the Best

Problem

Birbal constantly asserted that everything happens for one's own good. Emperor Akbar, who was young, was distrustful of Birbal's wisdom and questioned the minister's constant, optimistic assertion.

One day while handling a sword, the Emperor chopped off the tip of his little finger. Birbal immediately told the Emperor not to worry, everything that happens has a purpose behind it and that purpose is for good. The Emperor became exceedingly angry with Birbal and threw him in jail.

The Emperor bandaged the finger for a few days and then, as a diversion, went into the forest to hunt. He was later separated from his hunting party and eventually captured by a tribe of cannibals intending to make a human sacrifice. The Emperor was bound like a sacrificial lamb and taken before the temple. When the temple priest examined him, the priest announced that he could not be sacrificed because he was not a perfect specimen, since the front portion of one finger was missing. As he was not fit to be sacrificed, the Emperor was released.

On his return, the Emperor thanked God for injuring his finger and thereby sparing his life. He then immediately went to the prison to meet Birbal.

"O Birbal, please accept my apologies for imprisoning you. Now I understand how my injury was for the best. But tell me, why did God allow me to imprison you? How is it for the best that you have been confined here due to my anger?"

Birbal's Solution

Birbal replied, "Your Majesty, if I had not been in prison, you would surely have taken me with you when you went hunting, and when the forest cannibals rejected you for their sacrifice, they would surely have found me an excellent substitute!"

Management Moral: It is helpful to see the good side of what appear to be bad events. It is a morale booster; it is also an aid to creativity, since it spurs you on to bounce back from ill fortune and get on optimistically with your life.

Belief in a higher power added to the belief that this power has our best interests in mind can help us feel more centred or better anchored whether in our personal lives or in a high responsibility professional life.

■ ■ ■

5. List of Fools

One day an Arab merchant arrived at the Court of Akbar with a large consignment of horses of all ages and breeds and offered them for sale.

Akbar was very impressed with the quality of the horses, paid up the prices demanded for the ones he selected and ordered the merchant to send him some more of the best that he could find in Arabia. The merchant agreed and demanded an advance sum of Rs 2 lakhs for them. Akbar immediately ordered the Court treasurer to pay the amount and the merchant left promising to return as soon as he had acquired the horses, which had been ordered.

Problem

Some time later, Akbar asked Birbal to prepare a list of fools in his kingdom.

Birbal replied, "Your Majesty, I have already made one," and handed him a long list. Akbar was astonished to find that his own name headed the list.

Outraged, he shouted at Birbal, "How dare you put your Emperor's name in the list of fools!"

Birbal's Solution

Birbal replied evenly, "Last week Your Majesty gave Rs 2 lakhs to the Arab merchant without any guarantee that he would bring you the horses that you ordered and paid for. That justifies my putting your name at the top of the list of fools."

Akbar asked him, "What if the merchant brings me the horses which I have ordered?"

"Then, Your Majesty, I will replace your name with his."

Akbar realised he had made a mistake in advancing the money and remained silent.

Management Moral: *Don't take things at their face value and admit and learn from your mistakes even if you are shown up as a fool by your subordinates. Also, the ability to trust is necessary in business and professional life but one has to be selective about whom one puts his trust in. Judicious trust is an absolute must for both efficiency and effectiveness in management.*

■ ■ ■

6. Theft of Jewels

Problem

A merchant in Akbar's kingdom felt hot and decided to have a bath. He bundled up all the jewels he was wearing, left them in a corner of his room along with his clothes and went for a bath. When he came out from his bath, he discovered that his jewels had vanished. He questioned all his servants but was unable to discover who had stolen the jewels. He decided to go to Akbar to have his problem solved. Akbar assigned the case to Birbal. Birbal called the merchant and asked him to bring all his servants to the Court the next day.

Birbal's Solution

When they appeared before him, Birbal handed each of the servants a stick and told them: "I have given each of you a stick of the same length. But they are magic sticks. Whenever they are in the possession of a thief they grow exactly by one inch a day. If you have stolen your master's jewels, your stick will grow by one inch when you come back tomorrow. So take them home and bring them back here tomorrow, at the same time." He then dismissed the servants.

The next day when the Court had assembled and the merchant's servants arrived with their sticks, Birbal collected all the sticks and placed them next to each other. One stick was shorter by one inch. Birbal told the merchant, "The servant who brought this stick is the one who stole the jewels. He cut the stick so it would not show that it grew by one inch and he would not be caught."

He then told the servants, "These are not magic sticks but because you believed that they were, the guilty servant cut an inch off his stick."

Immediately, the servant who had stolen the jewels confessed and returned them.

Management Moral: *Problem solving becomes easier if you learn ways to read the minds of those with whom you deal. Birbal knew the servants were superstitious and would believe his story about the magic properties of the sticks.*

Rooting out unscrupulous elements or correcting the ways of such people of doubtful character is a great service to society and therefore a noble end. Playing on the gullible nature of such persons is an acceptable means to a noble end.

■ ■ ■

7. The Holy Book

Problem

Akbar once called Birbal and said to him, "Birbal, it is said in one of your Hindu Holy Books that Lord Vishnu one day heard the agonised cry of one of His elephants and rushed to his aid. Why would a God with so many servants at his disposal himself rush to the succour of the elephant?"

Birbal replied, "Your Majesty, give me a few days to answer your question."

The Emperor granted him the request.

Birbal's Solution

Birbal made a wax model of the Emperor's grandson and dressed him up in the grandson's clothes. He then told the servant in charge of the grandson to carry this doll out where the Emperor could see him and pretend to fall to the ground and throw the doll into the pond nearby, uttering a cry to draw the Emperor's attention. "If you do so, I shall reward you greatly."

The servant followed Birbal's instructions, threw the doll into the pond and himself pretended to fall to the ground, uttering a plaintive cry.

When the Emperor heard the cry and saw his grandson fall into the pond, he rushed and jumped into the pond to rescue him.

Birbal stepped out of the bushes and lent a helping hand to the Emperor as he came out of the pond, asking him, "How did Your Majesty jump to the rescue of your

27

grandson when you have so many servants to do the job for you? For the same reason Lord Vishnu rushes to save whoever seeks His help, because in his eyes all creatures are equally precious."

Management Moral: *It is important to have the right sense of priorities, especially in treating your employees first as human beings and only then as mere human resources. The degree of concern distinguishes a leader from a mere boss. Respect for life, whether human, animal or environmental, as a value can lead to enlightened human beings whose behaviour will be translated into enlightened management where values rank above profits.*

■ ■ ■

8. Truth and Falsehood

Problem

One day Akbar asked his courtiers if they could tell him the difference between truth and falsehood in three words or less. The courtiers looked at one another in bewilderment. "What about you, Birbal?" asked the Emperor. "I'm surprised that you too are silent."

"I'm silent because I want to give others a chance to speak," said Birbal.

"Nobody else has the answer," said the Emperor. "So go ahead and tell me what the difference between truth and falsehood is, in three words or less."

Birbal's Solution

"Four fingers," said Birbal.

"Four fingers?" asked the Emperor, perplexed.

"That's the difference between truth and falsehood, Your Majesty," said Birbal. "That which you see with your own eyes is the truth. That which you have only heard about might not be true. More often than not, it's likely to be false."

"That is right," said Akbar. "But what did you mean by saying the difference is four fingers?"

"The distance between one's eyes and one's ears is the width of four fingers, Your Majesty," said Birbal, grinning.

Management Moral: *The distinction between the truth revealed by observation and the unreliability of hearsay is important. But often what we think is observation is actually interpreted observation and therefore unreliable. For instance, we tend to judge a man or woman by the clothes they are wearing. It so happens, therefore, that confidence tricksters use this tendency to their advantage. People are taken in at parties they gatecrash because they are dressed in expensive clothes. It is important, therefore, to distinguish between first impressions and conclusions drawn from continuous observation over time.*

Thus it is necessary to realise that in reality too the line between truth and falsehood is at times narrower than four fingers – and reality and what looks like it are often difficult to distinguish. Yet unless a manager is capable of distinguishing the two, there could be serious errors in management.

■ ■ ■

9. The Camel's Crooked Neck

Problem

Emperor Akbar was very impressed with Birbal's wisdom and greatly enjoyed his quick wit. One fine morning when Akbar was especially pleased with Birbal, as a gesture of appreciation, he promised to reward him with many valuable and beautiful gifts.

However, many days passed, and there was still no sign of any gift. Birbal was quite disappointed with the Emperor.

Birbal's Solution

Then one day, when Akbar was strolling down the banks of river Yamuna with the ever-faithful Birbal at his side, he happened to notice a camel passing by. He asked Birbal why the neck of the camel was crooked. Birbal thought for a second and promptly replied that it might be because the camel may have forgotten to honour a promise. The holy books mention that those who break their word get punished with a crooked neck. Perhaps that was the reason for the camel's crooked neck.

Akbar remembered making a promise to Birbal of some valuable gifts and not honouring it. As soon as they returned to the palace, he immediately gave Birbal his justly deserved reward.

Management Moral: *Birbal always managed to get what he wanted without directly asking for it. It is useful to learn ways of planting ideas, which you want to see implemented, in other people's minds and make them think they are their own ideas. Then they will tend to act on them with greater zeal. Also, keeping promises is an important clue to your character. Someone who neglects his promises devalues his own character and other good character traits he may have are turned to naught in the eyes of his subordinates.*

■ ■ ■

10. Lost and Found

Problem

One day, when Akbar and Birbal were engaged in discussions, Birbal happened to pass a harmless comment about Akbar's sense of humour. But Emperor Akbar was in a foul mood and took great offence at this remark. He asked Birbal, his court-jester, friend and confidant, to not only leave the palace but also leave the precincts of the city of Agra. Birbal was terribly hurt at being banished.

A couple of days later, Akbar began to miss his best friend. He regretted his earlier decision of banishing him from the Court. He just could not do without Birbal and so sent out a search party to look for him. But Birbal had left town without letting anybody know of his destination. The soldiers searched high and low but were unable to find him anywhere.

Birbal's Solution

Then one day a wise saint visited the palace accompanied by two of his disciples. The disciples claimed that their teacher was the wisest man to walk the earth. Since Akbar was missing Birbal terribly he thought it would be a good idea to have a wise man who could keep him company. But he decided that he would first ascertain the holy man's wisdom.

The saint had bright sparkling eyes, a thick beard and long hair. The next day, when they came to visit the Court, Akbar informed the holy man that since he was the wisest man on earth, he would like to test him. All his ministers would put forward a question and if his answers were satisfactory, he would be made a minister. But if he failed, he would be beheaded. The saint answered that he had never claimed to be the wisest man on earth, even though other people seemed to think so. Nor was he eager to display his wisdom, but as he enjoyed answering questions, he was ready for the test.

One of the ministers, Raja Todar Mal, began the round of questioning. He asked, "Who is man's best friend on earth?" To which the wise saint replied, "His own good sense."

Next Faizi asked which was the most superior thing on earth? "Knowledge," answered the saint.

"Which is the deepest trench in the world?" asked Abul Fazl. And the saint answered, "A woman's heart."

"What is that which cannot be regained after it is lost?" questioned another courtier and the reply he received was: "Life."

"What is undying in music?" asked Court musician Tansen. The wise saint replied: "Notes." And then Tansen asked, "Which is the sweetest and most melodious voice at night-time?" And the answer he received was: "The voice that prays to God."

Maharaj Mansingh of Jaipur – who was a guest at the palace – asked, "What travels more speedily than the wind?" The saint replied that it was "Man's thought." Mansingh then asked, "Which is the sweetest thing on earth?" and the saint said that it was "a baby's smile".

Emperor Akbar and all his courtiers were very impressed with his answers, but Akbar wanted to test the saint himself. First, he asked what were the necessary requirements to rule over a kingdom, for which he received the response "Cleverness". Then he asked what was the greatest enemy of a king. The saint replied it was "Selfishness"

The Emperor was pleased and offered the saint a seat of honour and asked him whether he could perform any miracle. The saint said that he could manifest any person the Emperor wished to meet. Akbar was thrilled and immediately asked to meet his minister and best friend Birbal.

The saint simply pulled off his artificial beard and hair much to the surprise of the courtiers. Akbar was stunned and could not believe his eyes. He stepped down to embrace the saint because he was none other than Birbal!

Akbar had tears in his eyes as he told Birbal that he had suspected it was him and had therefore asked whether he could perform miracles. He showered Birbal with many valuable gifts to show him how happy he was at his return.

Management Moral: *Birbal knew Akbar so well that he could guess his thoughts and feelings. This ability is known as empathy. It is important to cultivate empathy with bosses, subordinates as well as customers. "How would I act if I were in their shoes?" This is a question that should be persistently asked in a business setting as well as in personal and family situations to establish strong ties with people. Your guess should then be checked against how the concerned person really acted in that situation. With practice empathy can be mastered.*

When we are victims of our superiors' injustice or have to bear the brunt of their temper undeservedly, it may pay off if we have a little patience rather than react impulsively. If we make an effort it is possible to take time to express our hurt and allow our superiors to backtrack without humiliating them. By saving their face it can only improve our relationship, instead of spoiling it further by having a confrontation.

■ ■ ■

11. The Washerman's 'Donkey'

Problem

One fine day Akbar, accompanied by his two sons and his clever minister Birbal, went to the river to take a bath. They asked Birbal to hold their clothes while they were bathing. They took off their clothes and stepped into the river.

Birbal stood at the bank of the river, waiting for them, with their clothes on his shoulder. Looking at Birbal standing like this, Akbar felt like teasing him and remarked that Birbal looked like a washerman's donkey with a load of clothes.

Birbal's Solution

Birbal quickly retorted that he was carrying the load of not just one donkey, but actually three.

The Emperor was speechless!

Management Moral: *Quick wit often helps you out of awkward situations. Birbal demonstrated to Akbar without stating in as many words that it was not proper for the Emperor to load his minister with his family's clothes. If the Emperor had remonstrated with him for showing disrespect to the Emperor, Birbal would have been ready with an appropriate answer.*

Birbal's wisdom emphasises the Biblical injunction: "Don't do unto others what you would not have others do unto you." This tenet could hold one in good stead while framing management rules for the people under you. Could you follow all the rules that you frame for others?

■ ■ ■

12. Controversial Brinjal

Problem

Emperor Akbar was discussing brinjals with Birbal. He told him what a delicious and nutritious vegetable it was. Much to Akbar's surprise, Birbal thoroughly agreed with him and even sang two songs in praise of the humble brinjal.

After a couple of days, the royal chef cooked brinjal curry for lunch. Birbal was also eating at the palace that day. When the brinjal curry was served to Akbar, he refused it saying that it was a tasteless, stale vegetable, full of seeds and lacking proper nutrition. He then asked that it be served to Birbal who loved brinjals.

But Birbal, too, refused it impatiently saying that it was not good for health. So Akbar asked him why he was saying such things, when he had actually sung the brinjal's praise only a few days ago.

Birbal's Solution

Birbal replied that he had praised the brinjal only because his Emperor had praised it and criticised it when His Majesty had criticised it, as he was loyal to his Emperor and not to the brinjal! Birbal said the brinjal could not make him a minister no matter how much he praised it.

The Emperor was pleased by the bold and witty response.

> **Management Moral:** *It is important to know what to say when. Inappropriate comments can have unsavoury repercussions. Such comments should be reserved for private moments, if at all called for. But it is never inappropriate to make your loyalty known to your boss. Besides, Birbal learns to make the best of whatever situation he is in – when appropriate he theoretically agreed with the Emperor that the brinjal was good and sang praises of the vegetable. Again he stuck to the Emperor's decision not to eat it and yet used the situation to his advantage claiming that he behaved in this way so as to be loyal to the Emperor.*

■ ■ ■

13. Akbar's Dream

Problem

One night, Emperor Akbar dreamt that he had lost all his teeth, except one. The next morning he invited all the astrologers of his kingdom to interpret this dream.

After long discussions, the astrologers prophesied that all the Emperor's relatives would die before him.

Akbar was very upset by this interpretation and sent away all the astrologers without any reward. Later that day, Birbal entered the Court. Akbar related his dream and asked him to interpret it.

Birbal's Solution

After thinking for a while, Birbal replied that the Emperor would live a longer and more fulfilled life than any of his relatives.

Akbar was pleased with Birbal's explanation and rewarded him handsomely.

Management Moral: *There is more than one way of expressing the truth. The worst shortcomings can be discussed with your subordinates without stepping on their corns or touching a raw nerve.*

If it becomes necessary to resort to a bitter pill in the course of your duty as a manager, there is always the option of using a sugar coating to soften the harshness – and it can turn out to be worthwhile!

What Birbal did is known as reframing. You form a judgement about a certain situation depending on the context in which you see it. You may see yourself as unjustly treated if you are overlooked for a promotion. But if you see your plight in the context of those who don't even have a job, though they are even more qualified than you, you will see yourself as lucky and more justly treated by fate than all these less fortunate people. It is a matter of seeing a glass as half full or half empty. The facts are the same. Your perception or interpretation can vary.

■ ■ ■

14. Shorter Line

Emperor Akbar's Court was famous for its witty question-and-answer sessions. On one occasion, the Emperor asked Birbal if there was anything that the sun and the moon could not see. Birbal's reply was: "Darkness."

Akbar was pleased.

Problem

Then, Emperor Akbar drew a line on the floor and asked Birbal to shorten it without wiping out the ends.

Birbal's Solution

Birbal drew a longer line below the line drawn by Akbar and remarked that though he had not rubbed off the original line he had definitely succeeded in making it the shorter of the two lines!

Management Moral: *There is usually a solution to every problem if you approach it from a new perspective. Birbal's answers to the problems he faced were never obvious, but seem very simple once they are known. It is a good exercise in creative thinking to try to think out your own answers to the problems put to Birbal before you read his solutions.*

By this very simplicity in his approach to quizzical questions, Birbal demonstrates that it does not take a genius to solve everyday problems and tricky situations. Giving all of your mind to it through undivided attention and a good dose of common sense normally does the trick.

■ ■ ■

15. The Eggs-ample

Problem

Since Birbal always outwitted him, Akbar thought of a plan to make Birbal look like a fool. He gave an egg to each of his ministers before Birbal reached the Court one morning.

So when Birbal arrived, the Emperor narrated a dream he had had the previous night saying that he would be able to judge the honesty of his ministers if they were able to bring back an egg from the royal garden pond.

So Akbar asked all his courtiers to go to the pond one at a time and return with an egg. One by one, all his ministers went to the pond and returned with an egg, which he had previously given them.

Birbal's Solution

Then it was Birbal's turn. He jumped into the pond and could find no eggs. He finally realised that the Emperor was trying to play a trick on him. So he entered the Court crowing like a cock.

The Emperor commanded him to stop making the irritating noise and asked him to produce the egg. Birbal smiled and replied that only hens lay eggs and as he was a cock, he could not produce an egg!

Everyone laughed loudly and the Emperor realised that Birbal could never be easily fooled.

Management Moral: The ability to turn awkward situations in your favour is an art worth cultivating. When you don't succeed, try to put yourself in the shoes of someone who usually does, and you may get ideas on how to succeed next time. If you were in Birbal's place, what other solution would you have thought of to outwit the Emperor? It is an exercise worth doing. Try to put yourself in Birbal's shoes in every situation narrated in this book and think of how you would have come out of it triumphantly.

On the other hand, if you are the boss throwing your weight around and trying to outsmart a brilliant subordinate, it may not work in your favour. Especially if you act as foolishly as Akbar and go to the extent of trying to make a fool of a smart and witty subordinate, you may inflict a similar experience upon yourself and end up at the receiving end of the joke – looking like a fool yourself, that too in front of all your staff!

■ ■ ■

16. Crows in the Kingdom

Problem

One day Emperor Akbar and Birbal were taking a walk in the palace gardens. It was a fine summer morning and there were plenty of crows enjoying themselves around the pond. While watching the crows, a question popped into Akbar's head. He wondered how many crows there were in his kingdom. Since Birbal was accompanying him, he asked Birbal this question.

Birbal's Solution

After a moment's thought, Birbal replied, "There are ninety-five thousand four hundred and sixty-three crows in the kingdom."

Amazed by his quick response, Akbar tried to test him again, "What if there are more crows than you mentioned?"

Without hesitating, Birbal replied, "If there are more crows than my answer, then it means some crows are visiting from neighbouring kingdoms."

"And what if there are less crows?" Akbar asked.

"Then some crows from our kingdom may have gone on holiday to other places!"

Management Moral: *Beware of statistics. They are often used to impress, but their reliability is often suspect. Even if the statistics are themselves correct, they can be variously interpreted. Likewise, results of laboratory tests are often interpreted differently by different experts. It is always safer to get a second opinion when confronted with statistics based upon which you have to take important decisions. Birbal used this opportunity to acquaint Akbar with this truth indirectly.*

Secondly, unless you have in place some mechanism for checking the performance of your subordinates or their efficiency, there is no point trying to quiz them about it. Without checks a great majority are bound to bluff their superiors. It is part of human nature.

■ ■ ■

17. Self-publicity

Problem

One day a Brahmin by the name of Sevaram asked Birbal for help. He said that his forefathers were great Sanskrit scholars and that people used to respectfully refer to them as Panditji. He said that he had no money nor need for wealth; he was content living a simple life. But he had just one wish. He wished people would refer to him as Panditji too. He asked Birbal how he could achieve this.

Birbal's Solution

Birbal said that the task was fairly simple. If the Brahmin followed his advice word for word, this task could be achieved. Birbal advised the Brahmin to shout at anyone who called him Panditji from now on.

Now the children who lived in the same street as the Brahmin did not like him since he scolded them often. They were just waiting for an opportunity to get back at him. Birbal told the children that the Brahmin would get really irritated if they started calling him Panditji. So the children began to tease him by yelling "Panditji" whenever he appeared and, as advised by Birbal, the Brahmin responded by shouting at them. The children spread the word to all the other children in the neighbourhood that Sevaram hated being called Panditji, so they too joined in the chorus, calling him Panditji.

After a while, Sevaram got tired of scolding them but by now everyone was used to calling him Panditji. Hence the game was over but the name stuck!

Management Moral: *If you want something about you widely known, make it known to gossips who will do your work for you free, particularly if you give it a newsy twist! For your purpose, today's equivalent of the urchins who lived in Akbar's time is the Press. Have you received a little-known award lately? Write it up, giving the background and importance of the award and send it to newspapers and periodicals. Many of them will lap it up, particularly if you are sufficiently important in your organisation or community.*

Another moral we can draw from the story: There are many ways of getting respect from society or your subordinate. You can command it by your behaviour or exemplary life; demand it especially if you are a powerful person; or lust after it but just pretend you don't want the respect and then trick the urchins into addressing you respectfully like Sevaram. Only, at the outset we have to decide the best way for us – which way can give us satisfaction and which way would Sevaram feel more respected. By playing a trick or by studying in order to become a learned scholar like his forefathers?

■ ■ ■

18. Three Questions

Problem

Emperor Akbar was very fond of Birbal. This made a certain courtier very jealous. Now this courtier always wanted to be the chief minister, but this was not possible as Birbal filled that position.

One day Akbar praised Birbal in front of the courtier. This made the courtier very angry and he said that the Emperor had praised Birbal without any basis and if Birbal could answer three of his questions, he would accept the fact that Birbal was intelligent. Akbar, who always enjoyed testing Birbal's wit, readily agreed.

The three questions were:

1. How many stars are there in the sky?
2. Where is the centre of the Earth?
3. How many men and women are there in the world?

Immediately Akbar asked Birbal the three questions and informed him that if he could not answer them, he would have to resign as Chief Minister.

Birbal's Solution

To answer the first question, Birbal brought a hairy sheep and said, "There are as many stars in the sky as there is hair on the sheep's body. My friend, the courtier is welcome to count them if he likes."

To answer the second question, Birbal drew a couple of lines on the floor, bore an iron rod in-between and said: "This is the centre of the Earth, the courtier may measure it himself if he has any doubts."

In answer to the third question, Birbal said: "Counting the exact number of men and women in the world would be a problem as there are some specimens like our courtier friend here who cannot easily be classified as either. Therefore, if all people like him are killed, then and only then can one count the exact number of men and women."

Management Moral: *It often happens that some inefficient people try to supplant efficient and capable people by questioning their efficiency. This tactic overloads them and undermines their efficiency while at the same time it hides the laziness and incapability of the shirkers. On such occasions, a little wit can go a long way in putting unscrupulous elements in their place.*

■ ■ ■

19. Birbal's Khichri

Problem

On a cold winter day, Akbar and Birbal took a walk along the lake. A thought came into Birbal's mind that a man would do anything for money. He expressed his feelings to Akbar. The Emperor then put his finger into the lake and immediately removed it because he shivered with cold.

Akbar said, "I don't think a man would spend an entire night in the cold water of this lake for money."

Birbal replied, "I am sure I can find such a person."

Akbar then challenged Birbal to find such a person and said he would reward that person with a thousand gold coins.

Birbal searched far and wide until he found a poor man who was desperate enough to accept the challenge. The poor man entered the lake and Akbar had guards posted near him to make sure that he really did as promised.

The next morning the guards took the poor man to Akbar. The Emperor asked the poor man if he had indeed spent the night in the lake. The poor man replied that he had. Akbar then asked the poor man how he managed to spend the night in the lake. The poor man replied that there was a street lamp nearby and he kept his attention fixed on the lamp and away from the cold. Akbar then said that there would be no reward as the poor man had survived the night in the lake by the warmth of the street lamp. The poor man went to Birbal for help.

Birbal's Solution

The next day, Birbal did not go to the Court. Wondering where he was, the Emperor sent a messenger to his home. The messenger came back saying that Birbal would come once his khichri was cooked. The Emperor waited for hours but Birbal did not come. Finally, Akbar decided to go to Birbal's house and see what he was up to.

He found Birbal sitting on the floor near some burning twigs and a utensil filled with khichri hanging five feet above the fire. The Emperor and his attendants couldn't help but laugh.

Akbar then asked Birbal, "How can the khichri be cooked if it is so far away from the fire?"

Birbal answered, "The same way the poor man received heat from a street lamp that was more than a furlong away."

The Emperor realised his mistake and gave the poor man his reward.

Management Moral: *Example is more effective than argument in any communication. If you have to explain your point of view in a presentation, it will meet with much better understanding if you use dramatic examples than if you use long-winding arguments to support it. There's a difference between making mistakes from lack of knowledge and making mistakes for our convenience. Our faulty behaviour becomes even more deplorable when we know that our 'convenient mistakes' trample on the well-being and basic comfort of others and yet we stubbornly hold on to our behaviour pattern and have no scruples about causing misery to others as our own convenience comes first.*

■ ■ ■

20. Poet Raidas

Problem

In the town of Agra lived a rich businessman. But he was also a miser. Various people used to flock outside his house everyday hoping for some kind of generosity, but they always had to return home disappointed. He used to ward them off with false promises, never living up to his word.

Then one day, a poet named Raidas arrived at his house and said that he wanted to read out his poems to the rich man. As the rich man was very fond of poetry, he welcomed him with open arms.

Raidas then recited all his poems one by one. The rich man was very pleased and especially so when he heard the poem that Raidas had written on him, because he had been compared with Kubera, the god of wealth. In those days it was a custom for rich men and kings to show their appreciation through a reward or gift, as that was the only means of earning for a poor poet. So the rich man promised Raidas some gifts and asked him to come and collect them the next day. Raidas was pleased.

The next morning when the poet arrived at the house, the rich man pretended that he had never laid eyes on him before. When Raidas reminded him of his promise, he said that although Raidas was a good poet he understood very little of human nature. And that if a rich businessman like him truly wanted to reward the poet, he would have done so the very same night. Raidas had been offered a reward not because he was really pleased or impressed, but simply to encourage him.

Raidas was extremely upset, but as there was nothing that he could do, he quietly left the house. On his way home he saw Birbal riding a horse. So he stopped him and asked for his help after narrating the whole incident.

Birbal's Solution

Birbal took him to his own house in order to come up with a plan. After giving it some thought he asked Raidas to go to a friend's house and request the friend to plan a dinner on the coming full moon night, where the rich man would also be invited. Birbal then asked Raidas to relax and leave the rest to him.

Raidas had a trusted friend whose name was Mayadas. So he went up to him and told him the plan. The next day, Mayadas went to the rich man's house and invited him for dinner. The dinner had been planned for the coming full moon night. Mayadas said that he intended to serve his guests in vessels of gold, which the guests would get to take home after the meal. The rich man was thrilled to hear this and jumped at the offer.

After sunset on the full moon night, the rich man arrived at Mayadas' house and was surprised to see no other guests there except Raidas. Anyway, they welcomed him and began a polite conversation. The rich man had come on an empty stomach and so was getting hungrier by the minute. Raidas and Mayadas were quite full, as they had eaten just before the rich man's arrival.

Finally, at midnight, the rich man could bear his hunger no longer and asked Mayadas to serve the food. Mayadas sounded extremely surprised and asked him what food he was talking about! The rich man tried to remind him that he had been invited for dinner. At this point Raidas asked him for proof of the invitation. The rich man had no answer. Then Mayadas told him that he had just invited him to please him and had not really meant it. He then went on to say that even though they did not do anything good for other people, they also would never try to hurt another human being. He asked the rich man not to feel bad.

At that point Birbal walked into the room and reminded the rich man of the same treatment that he had himself meted out to Raidas. The rich man realised his mistake and begged for forgiveness. He said that Raidas was a good poet and had not asked him for any reward. He himself had promised to give him some gifts and then cheated him out of them. To make up for his mistake he took out the necklace that he was wearing and gifted it to Raidas. Then they all sat down to eat a hearty meal.

Raidas was all praise for Birbal and thanked him profusely. Emperor Akbar also invited Raidas to his Court and honoured him, all thanks to Birbal.

Management Moral: *If you want to convince someone of your plight, put him in your shoes. Birbal put the rich man in the poet's position, making him experience hunger at first hand before he showed him the error of his miserly ways.*

If you are a man of principles, you are bound to consider justice as one of the important tenets in all your dealings. Very often we get back in a larger measure whatever we dish out. By making amends at a late stage not all unpleasant consequences can be avoided – not for ourselves, and certainly not for our victims. Besides, our ways are very likely to become known to others and be a cause of embarrassment and shame.

■ ■ ■

21. The Emperor's Whiskers

Problem

One day Emperor Akbar startled his courtiers with a strange question. "If somebody pulled my whiskers, what sort of punishment should be meted out to him?" he asked.

"He should be flogged!" said one courtier.

"He should be hanged!" said another.

"He should be beheaded!" said a third.

"And what about you, Birbal?" asked the Emperor. "What do you think would be the right thing to do if somebody pulled my whiskers?"

Birbal's Solution

"He should be given sweets," said Birbal.

"Sweets?" gasped the other courtiers.

"Yes," said Birbal. "Sweets, because the only one who would dare pull His Majesty's whiskers is his grandson."

So pleased was the Emperor with the answer that he pulled off his ring and gave it to Birbal as a reward.

Management Moral: *The right solution to a problem can usually be found in the context. If somebody's behaviour appears inexplicable to you, question the person in depth and the explanation will probably turn out to be quite reasonable. Different people see things from different perspectives. The Emperor's grandchild will see his grandfather's whiskers differently from a* *courtier. Likewise, different customers may see your products differently. Seeing these products from their point of view will help you appreciate their needs and improve your product or service.*

Besides, whereas in the case of a courtier such behaviour (pulling the Emperor's whiskers) would be an affront, the same behaviour on his young grandson's part would be considered affectionate.

This is a classic case of propriety and context where one's behaviour is concerned. So also propriety is the key when you live in the corporate world – one wrong phrase at a meeting could destroy your chances of advancement; and whereas too much familiarity with your professional associates may not be proper, a lack of warmth or insufficient familiarity may work against you. Like everything else in life, it's the balance that counts.

■ ■ ■

22. Retrieving the Ring

Problem

Once Akbar threw his gold ring into a dry well and asked his ministers to retrieve it without climbing down into the well.

The ministers scratched their heads and thought deeply but soon had to admit defeat. Birbal, however, could never resist a challenge.

"Jahanpanah, you shall get back your ring before sundown," he declared.

Birbal's Solution

Birbal took some fresh cow-dung from the ground and threw it on top of the ring. He then tied a stone to one end of a long piece of string and retaining the other end, threw the stone on the dung. After a while, when he felt sure that the cow-dung had dried completely, he pulled the string up. To everyone's surprise the cow-dung came up and stuck at the bottom was the Emperor's ring.

Management Moral: *If you exercise your imagination, develop enough interest and motivation to face every challenge and allow your creativity to always blossom, no problem will be too difficult to solve.*

In spite of all the management courses and HRD/ personality training programmes that we can avail of in the present day, we may not be able to match the wisdom of Birbal in creative problem solving nor the countless opportunities Akbar could provide his ministers with to build up their creativity and problem-solving abilities. Why were they different from the present-day managers? Each one has to come up with his/her own answer to this question, in order to grasp the moral in its totality. Our clues are again rhetorical questions like: Are modern managers too smug in their jobs? Do they have to give off their best?

■ ■ ■

23. Astrologer's Woes

Problem

Emperor Akbar had heard that a certain astrologer was boasting that he was never wrong in his predictions. He had him brought to the Court to punish him.

"You say you can foretell the future accurately," Akbar said to the terrified man. "Tell me when you will die."

The man said he had to consult his charts and the Emperor gave him an hour to do so. But instead of consulting his charts, the astrologer consulted Birbal, who told him what he should say.

Birbal's Solution

Returning to the Court, the astrologer announced that according to his calculations he would die three days before the Emperor.

Akbar suspected that the man was bluffing but was so frightened by the prospect of dying soon after the astrologer that he sent him away unharmed.

Management Moral: *Often it is possible to get the better of people by exploiting their fears. If the astrologer had predicted any other date for his own death, Akbar could have ordered him put to death at an earlier time just to prove him wrong. Fear can cloud your judgement and thwart your plans. If you dream of accomplishing a lot, learn first to banish your unreasonable fears and act with a clear mind.*

Another moral you can draw from the story is that the results of overconfidence and arrogance can be disastrous. Akbar did not like the astrologer's boasting nor do our superiors like it when their staff are overconfident and brag a lot. The astrologer had to fall back on Birbal's advice to get himself out of a near-fatal situation. If we put ourselves in such a situation, we may not be able to find such a timely saviour.

■ ■ ■

24. The Well Water

Problem

A farmer and his neighbour once went to Emperor Akbar's Court with a complaint.

"Your Majesty, I bought a well from him," said the farmer pointing to his neighbour, "and now he wants me to pay for the water."

"That's right, Your Majesty," said the neighbour. "I sold him the well but not the water!"

The Emperor asked Birbal to settle the dispute.

Birbal's Solution

"Didn't you say that you sold your well to this farmer?" Birbal asked the neighbour. "So the well belongs to him now, but you have kept your water in his well. Is that right? Well, in that case you will have to pay him rent or take your water out at once."

The neighbour realised that he was outwitted. He quickly apologised and gave up his claim.

Management Moral: *If you don't give people their due, you may be the loser. They may feel provoked to take away more than their due – even what is rightfully yours! Whenever you draft or sign an agreement make sure all clauses are clear and that there is no scope for costly and time-consuming litigation. If you know that any of your practices is not fair or ethical, whether towards your client, competitor or employee, it may* *not be to your advantage to pursue it just because there has not been any past ruling on the matter. You will not enjoy being sued and becoming the subject of a new court ruling especially if your opponent gets the chance to turn you into a victim.*

■ ■ ■

25. The Pandit's Pot

Problem

A pandit once went to Akbar's Court and told the Emperor he would like to test the intelligence of his courtiers. Akbar gave him permission. The courtiers gathered in the palace at the appointed hour. The pandit kept a covered pot before them and asked them to tell him what it contained.

Birbal's Solution

There was absolute silence. Then Birbal stepped forward. He uncovered the pot and said there was nothing in it.

"But you opened it!" said the pandit.

"You did not say we could not open it," replied Birbal. The pandit was disappointed. He bowed to the Emperor and walked away.

Management Moral: *Very often our mind invents obstacles that do not exist. Don't assume rules that don't exist. The obvious solution often escapes the excessively preoccupied mind. Cultivate a mind that gets to the nub of an issue.*

Also, never underestimate the potential and capability of people around you. Each of us has our own resources.

■ ■ ■

26. Akbar's Cloak

Several courtiers were vying for the post of Royal Advisor. The Emperor said he would put them to the test and the one who passed the test would be appointed to the post.

Problem

So saying, Akbar unfastened his cloak and lay on the floor. He then challenged the courtiers to cover him from head to toe with the cloak.

One by one the courtiers tried, but their attempts proved futile. If the head was covered, the feet remained exposed. And vice versa. Some even tried pulling and tugging at the cloak but in vain.

Birbal's Solution

Just then Birbal entered. The Emperor asked Birbal if he could do it. Birbal took the cloak and then looked at the Emperor lying on the floor.

"Jahanpanah, would you kindly draw up your knees?" he said. The Emperor drew up his knees. Birbal then threw the cloak over him and it covered him from head to toe.

Realising that they had failed the test, the courtiers quietly filed out of the room.

Management Moral: *A rigid mind may not be able to utilise the available resources to the best capacity. Once the mind turns flexible, it can solve problems more easily. Merely a certificate confirming the student's qualifications, whether it is graduation, post-graduation or management, should not be all you need to appoint a candidate to an opening in your office. One of the basic criteria could be the capacity of the candidate in relation to the demands and nature of the vacancy to be filled. Have we developed foolproof tests like Akbar?*

■ ■ ■

27. Making the Line Vanish

Problem

Birbal developed a new interest in geometry, but did not tell anyone about it. One day he received a message that Akbar had called him to the Court. The Sultan of Persia had sent the wisest man in his kingdom to Akbar's Court and he had a puzzle for every courtier. Birbal had been summoned after everyone else had failed to solve it.

"Only a magician can do it," said Raja Maan Singh, after spending two hours trying to find a solution.

"What challenge do you have for us?" Birbal asked the wise man from Persia.

"Simple! I have drawn 10 equally spaced vertical lines. Make any one of these vanish without cutting or rubbing off any of these," said the wise man.

Birbal's Solution

Birbal smiled and examined the vertical lines of equal length drawn on a sheet of paper. He drew a diagonal from the bottom of the first line to the top of the tenth line and cut the sheet along it. He slid the lower piece of the paper downward and to the left until there were only nine lines on the paper. The tenth line just vanished.

"Hail Raja Birbal! Hail Raja Birbal!" said all the courtiers.

"Wonderful! Bravo Birbal, bravo! We are proud of you," Akbar said.

"You," Akbar addressed the Persian scholar, "never dare challenge an Indian again."

"Yes, Your Majesty, I will remember what you have just said," the scholar remarked.

"However, where has the missing line gone Birbal?" asked Akbar.

"Mahabali, believe it or not, a part of it has became a part of each of the other lines," Birbal replied and smiled again, while the Emperor and the courtiers wondered.

Problem

Just then, a poor farmer stood out of the crowd and bowed before the Emperor. "Huzoor, I have a problem as well, can Raja Birbal help me solve it?" he queried.

"Let all of us know what puzzle you have for Birbal; say it aloud," said Akbar.

The farmer said, "Sire, I have five pigs, but only enough material to build four pens – 16 lengths of fence material to make four four-sided enclosures. If I put two pigs in any one pen, one pig will climb on the other pig's back and hop out of the pen. He will then open all the other pens with his snout. I cannot sell or kill the pigs because they are my daughter's pets and extremely intelligent as well. How can I get these five pigs into four pens?"

"Would any other courtier like to try it, before I request Birbal to do so?" Akbar asked. Several volunteers raised their hands. Each one of them was given 16 straws representing the 16 lengths of fence material. They had to solve the problem without putting more than one pig into any pen and without cutting any of the fences as the material was the bare minimum.

Birbal's Solution

When the volunteers gave up, Birbal showed them the solution. He made a central pen, each wall of which was shared by one of the other four pens. Thus, the farmer saved the four extra lengths of fence material required to build the fifth enclosure.

Management Moral 1: *The merit of a person lies in his abilities. When you know you have them, there is no need to feel intimidated about lending your know-how to any foreigner or foreign country, howsoever powerful.*

Management Moral 2: *Save through sharing – space, material, time, ideas!*

■ ■ ■

28. Greater Than God?

One day, two poets from a faraway kingdom arrived at the Court. They delighted everyone with their songs and poems. The Emperor, who was always generous, rewarded them well. The poets had never seen so much gold before. They were overwhelmed. Then the Emperor ordered that they be given a set of princely clothes each.

Then one of the poets begged permission to offer a poem of thanks. Emperor Akbar nodded and the poet began his recitation. He spoke of the Emperor's bravery and kindness. He praised the Emperor's learning and wisdom.

He ended by saying that Emperor Akbar was the greatest king that had ever ruled "over this world or any other. He is greater than God Himself." With that, the poet bowed and left the hall.

There was a moment of silence. Many of those in the hall were shocked that the poet had compared a mortal to God.

Problem

Emperor Akbar looked around and his eyes began to twinkle mischievously. "So," he said, "it appears that I am now even greater than God."

All the people in the hall looked at their Emperor in horror. Had he really believed the poet's words? Surely not! And yet, they were not entirely sure. Emperor Akbar looked at his ministers and commanders, his nobles and his counsellors. He wondered if any of them would have the courage to speak the truth. The ministers, commanders, nobles and counsellors looked back at him. Nobody stirred.

"So," said the Emperor, beginning to feel irritated, "everyone present agrees that your Emperor is greater than God."

Nobody dared to disagree. Slowly, one by one, the courtiers bowed to show that they agreed. A low, shamed murmur of "Yes, Your Majesty," "It is so, Your Majesty," filled the hall.

Emperor Akbar thought that the courtiers were acting very foolishly. He turned to Birbal with a frown. "And you, Birbal. Do you agree too?" he asked.

Birbal's Solution

"Oh, yes," Birbal replied immediately.

The Emperor's frown grew.

"Your Majesty, you can do something even God cannot!" Birbal said. "If any of your subjects displeases you, Your Majesty, you can send him on a pilgrimage or banish him from your empire, never to return. But God cannot. For God rules over the entire earth and the sky and the heavens. There is no place in this world or any other that does not belong to God. So he cannot banish any of his creatures."

Emperor Akbar's frown vanished. "Well said, Birbal!" he cried delightedly. And, from every corner of the Court, relieved courtiers began to smile weakly and then laugh. Birbal had done it again!

Management Moral: *Never belittle your boss, but when you praise him, make the praise credible. This is not all that difficult. Even if your superiors know their shortcomings, it will not be appreciated if you adhere to your sincerity and confirm such shortcomings or dish out false praise – it would be wiser to evade such questions and focus on their positive characteristics, about which you may praise them as effusively as you want to!*

■ ■ ■

29. The Pot of Intelligence

Akbar had great confidence in Birbal. Once, for some unknown reason, the Emperor was not very happy with him. Sensing this, Birbal decided to stay away from the Emperor for a few days. He went to a small village and started living there.

Problem

One day, Akbar got a letter. One of his vassals, Raja Samant, had written, "Please send a pot full of intelligence."

Akbar could not comprehend what it meant. He thought, "If only Birbal was here, he would have explained it in a minute."

The Emperor came up with an idea to find out where Birbal might be. He invited the heads of the villages nearby and said, "I shall give a goat to each one of you. You must feed them well. Take good care of them. The cost is my responsibility. You must return the goats after one month. But when you return, the goats should weigh the same as they are today."

The village heads wondered how this would be possible.

Somehow, Birbal came to know about this. He went to see the Patel (village head).

Birbal's Solution

"Patelji, do not worry about what the Emperor has said. Just take good care of the goat," said Birbal.

"In that case, the goat will grow fat."

"There is a solution for that. On the outskirts of the village, you have seen that lion in the cage. Tie up this goat just a little way off from the lion. Due to fear and insecurity, the goat will not gain an ounce of weight," said Birbal.

The Patel followed Birbal's instructions. After a month all the goats were brought to the Emperor. Only one goat had not gained any weight. Akbar guessed that this was possible only with Birbal's help. He sent for Birbal and pacified him. Then he said, "Birbal, I need your advice. How can I send a pot full of intelligence to someone?"

Birbal started working on it. First, he got a pot, filled it with soil and sowed a pumpkin seed in it. It sprouted and a pumpkin grew inside the pot. When the pumpkin filled the pot Birbal cut off the plant. The pumpkin remained inside the pot. Birbal tied a cloth and covered the pot. He showed this to Akbar.

"O Sire, send this to Raja Samant with a letter. Say, 'This pot is full of intelligence. Take it out carefully. While removing the pumpkin, the pot should not break and the container should not get damaged. If anything contrary to this happens, you will have to pay a very heavy penalty.'"

The vassal received the pot and the letter. He realised what an impossible task it was. He came to Akbar's Court and apologised. He realised what a fool he was to ask for a pot of intelligence from an Emperor in whose kingdom a man like Birbal lived!

Management Moral: *Most problems have solutions. If you can't find them yourself, find someone who can! On the other hand, if you are as good as Birbal, make your abilities known, and become indispensable to your employer. As is obvious, your services will always be in demand and your prosperity will keep increasing.*

■ ■ ■

30. God in a Ring

Problem

Emperor Akbar once asked his wise Minister Birbal, "Well, Birbal, you often say God is everywhere."

Birbal reiterated, "Yes, Badshah! God is everywhere. There is absolutely no doubt in this."

Akbar pulled a diamond ring off his finger and asked Birbal, "Is your God in this ring, too?"

Birbal replied, "Yes, Badshah! He is certainly in the ring."

"Then can you make me see Him?" asked the Emperor.

Birbal had no answer to this. He asked for time. The Emperor allowed him six months to find an answer or a way to show Akbar God in the ring.

Solution

Birbal went home; he was puzzled. He knew there was a solution to the problem; but he knew not what. He dared not face the Emperor again without an answer to his question. He grew pale and anxious.

Shortly after this encounter with the Emperor, a little boy-mendicant came to Birbal's house for alms. He asked Birbal, "What ails you, Sir? Why do you look so sullen and miserable? You are a wise man, and wise men should have no reason for misery! Joy and tranquillity are the marked characteristics of a wise man."

"True!" replied Birbal: "The heart is convinced, but the intellect cannot frame words for it."

Birbal then narrated all that had transpired between him and the Emperor.

"Is this what you are worrying about?" exclaimed the boy in amazement. "I can give you the answer in a moment; but will you allow me to talk to the Emperor personally?"

Birbal replied in the affirmative and took the boy to the Imperial Court and addressed the Emperor, "My Lord! Even this little boy can give you the answer to your question."

Akbar inwardly appreciated the pluck and boldness of the boy and was curious to hear him. He asked the boy, "If God is all-pervading, son, can you show me your God in the ring?"

"O Sire!" replied the boy, "I can do so in a second, but I am thirsty. I can answer the question after I have taken a glass of curd."

The Emperor at once had a glassful of curd given to him. The boy began to stir the curd and said, "O Emperor, I am used to drinking good curd which has butter in it. I do not like this stuff which your bearer has brought and which does not yield butter at all."

"Certainly, this curd is the best available," replied the Emperor. "Remember, little one, that you are partaking of the product from the Emperor's personal dairy."

The boy said, "Very well! If Your Majesty is so sure that this cup of curd contains butter in it, please show me the butter."

The Emperor laughed aloud and said, "I thought so! O ignorant child! You do not even know that butter is obtained from curd only after churning it; and yet you have the audacity to come here to show me God!"

"I am not a fool, O Badshah," replied the boy quickly. "I only gave you the answer to your own question!"

The Emperor was puzzled. The boy said to him, "Your Majesty, in exactly the same manner the Lord resides within everything. He is the in-dwelling Presence, the Self of all, the Light of all lights, the Power that maintains the universe. Yet one cannot see Him with one's physical eyes. A vision is only a projection of one's own mind before the eye of the mind. One can realise God intuitively and see Him with the eye of wisdom. But before that one has to churn the five sheaths, and the objects, and separate the butter, the Reality, from the curd, the names and forms."

The young boy had thus answered Akbar's question and the Emperor was greatly impressed. He wanted to know more and asked, "Child! Now tell me, what is your God doing all the while?"

The boy-mendicant replied: "Well, Your Majesty, it is God who lends power to our senses, perception to our mind, discernment to our intellect, strength to our limbs; it is through His will that we live and die. But man vainly imagines that he is the actor and the enjoyer. Man is a mere nothing before the Almighty governing Power that directs movement in the universe.

"It is in the twinkling of an eye, when compared to the unimaginable age of the universe, that empires rise and fall, dynasties rise and perish, the boundaries of the land and the sea wax and wane, and we find a mountain range where there had been a sea and a new sea where there had been a plateau. It is in the twinkling of an eye that we find millionaires become paupers and paupers become millionaires. And a King becomes a wandering exile by a tryst of destiny and a vagrant becomes a King. So many planets are created, sustained and dissolved every moment in this vast universe. Who is behind this gigantic phenomena? It is God and none but the one God to realise whom one has to give up vanity, the feeling of doership, arrogance and pride. To realise Him one has to surrender oneself entirely to His will, which can be discerned through cultivation of purity, emotional maturity and intellectual conviction. To realise that God one has to efface oneself in toto and feel that one is a mere instrument of His will."

It was a new experience for Emperor Akbar to hear the ancient wisdom from so young a mendicant. Akbar was very liberal in his views, and this encounter with a Hindu child-monk was perhaps in a way partly responsible for the Emperor inviting to his Court many Hindu scholars and holy men to participate in spiritual and academic deliberations with Muslim fakirs and Maulvis.

Management Moral: *Look for wisdom in the most unlikely source; that is where it is most likely to be found.*

However smart you may be, even as smart as Birbal, there may come a time when you just can't get the right solution to a problem. But that does not mean that the problem has no answer. The answer may come easily if you are humble enough to discuss the problem with a wise subordinate or to have a brainstorming session with a few trusted colleagues and acknowledge that help is welcome.

Birbal's humility in allowing the young mendicant to speak to the Emperor about a solution to his problem fostered Akbar's appreciation of the child-monk's wisdom and godly knowledge and his future association with Hindu scholars at the Court. The story also strongly illustrates the communal harmony prevalent in Akbar's Court, which we could try to foster in our daily lives and in office set-ups.

■ ■ ■

31. The Effect of Your Actions

Problem

One day Akbar was simply chatting with his friends... And he had around him the very best, wisest, most creative people chosen from every part of the country. They were speaking, Akbar slapped Birbal – for no apparent reason. Now one could not slap the Emperor back, but the slap had to go somewhere.

Birbal's Solution

So Birbal slapped the person who was standing right next to him.

Everybody thought, "This is strange!"

There was no reason in the first place for Akbar's slap. Suddenly, as if some madness had seized Akbar, he had slapped poor Birbal. And the victim also reacted strangely. Rather than asking, "Why have you slapped me?" he simply slapped the man by his side! And that man, thinking perhaps this was the norm at the Court, slapped the next person. In a chain reaction, the slap went all around the Court.

That night, Akbar's wife slapped him! And he asked, "Why are you slapping me?"

She said, "What a question – a game is a game."

He said, "Who told you that this is a game?"

She said, "We have been hearing the whole day long that a great game has begun in the Court. The only rule is you cannot hit the person back, you have to find somebody else to slap. And somebody has slapped me – so your slap has come back to you. The game is now complete!"

Management Moral: *All kinds of fashions, fads and practices have strange, unexpected beginnings. A small gesture can have snowballing consequences. In this big world, thousands of insane games are going on in which we are all participants. The slap (or for that matter a good deed) is going to come back to you sooner or later. Where else will it go? Good deeds will bring you its rewards, however unexpected, and your misdeeds will eventually get you the punishment you deserve.*

Perhaps you have forgotten when you started it all. The world is big; it takes time to return. But everything comes back to its source – that is one of the fundamental rules of life, not just the rule of any game.

■ ■ ■

32. Akbar Learns a Lesson

Problem

Akbar always aspired to be a good administrator. He thought that as an Emperor he did not always get the true picture of his kingdom and subjects. He felt the need to see the condition of his kingdom and subjects as a lay person. And so he often disguised himself and wandered about Agra.

His minister, Birbal, did not approve of this as he thought it unsafe. On one such occasion when the disguised Emperor was getting ready to leave, Birbal expressed his disapproval, "Jahanpanah, this is not right. An Emperor's life is precious and must be well protected."

But Akbar didn't take heed of Birbal's warnings and stepped out onto the street.

Birbal's Solution

After a while, Akbar felt he was being followed. For some time he tried to shake off the pursuer. But when he couldn't, he decided to confront the man.

"What's your name?" asked Akbar.

"Wanderlust," replied the man.

"What do you do for a living?" asked Akbar.

"I wander," replied the man.

"Where do you live?" asked Akbar.

"Everywhere," pat came the reply.

By now Akbar was truly irritated, "Do you know who you are speaking with?"

"Yes, a human being, I guess," replied the stranger.

"No ordinary being. I am the Emperor. If you do not believe me take a look at my Seal." So saying the Emperor handed over the Seal to the man. At first the stranger peered at it. Then he quickly slipped it into his pocket and ran away.

Only then Akbar realised what he had done.

"Thief! Thief! Catch him! Catch him!" he called out in desperation.

A bunch of people heard his cries and followed the thief.

"Don't let him get away!" Akbar called out.

The people grabbed the stranger, who tried to shake them off saying, "Fools! Don't you know me? I am the Emperor. Take a look at my Seal, perhaps you will be convinced then."

The people were dumbfounded and humbly begged forgiveness.

"Forgive us, Jahanpanah, we were acting on the call of a madman."

Akbar watched all this in dismay. "I must return to the palace before they attack me," he thought to himself. "I'm sure Birbal can help me nab the thief. Birbal had warned me not to go out alone. Oh! How will I face him?"

Thinking of all this Akbar entered his chamber. As he did so, he noticed a parcel on the side table. Opening it he was shocked to see his Seal and a note.

The note read: "I have often warned you that it is not safe for you to venture out alone without your guards. Today you only lost your Seal, but worse things could have happened to you."

The note was signed, *Birbal*.

"So it was Birbal. Ha! Ha! But I have learnt my lesson, thanks to him," thought Akbar, once again grateful to his wise minister.

Management Moral: *Don't act impetuously. Think carefully of the consequences of your action before taking an important decision. The counsel of a wise officer or colleague is bound to have something in it. It is advisable not to discard it without giving it a second thought – else your actions may land you in dire straits.*

■ ■ ■

33. Call Him At Once

Problem

One morning Akbar woke up early. Rubbing his fingers over his stubble he called out, "Is anyone there? Quick! Call him at once!"

The guard outside his chamber was thoroughly confused. He thought to himself, "Whom is the Emperor calling, he didn't name anybody in particular." The guard was too frightened to ask the Emperor to repeat his order.

The guard sought the help of another guard. That guard in turn spoke to a third. The third mentioned it to a fourth. Finally all the guards inside the palace knew of the Emperor's order. There was utter confusion, as nobody knew whom the Emperor had called for.

Birbal's Solution

At that time Birbal happened to be taking a walk in the garden. Seeing the guards in total confusion, he guessed the Emperor must have made a strange request. He called one of the guards and asked him, "What is the matter? Why are all the guards running around confused?"

The guard told Birbal about the Emperor's order. He said, "His Majesty has not mentioned anyone in particular. Whom should we call? We do not know what to do. If we do not get anyone, the Emperor will be very annoyed with us. What shall we do, Sir?"

"Hmmm! Tell me what the Emperor was doing when he gave the order," asked Birbal.

The attendant pondered a while, "Nothing unusual Sir, he was just rubbing the stubble on his chin."

Birbal smiled for he knew whom the Emperor wanted. He said to the guard, "Take the barber to the Emperor immediately."

The guard called the barber and took him immediately to the Emperor. The Emperor thought to himself, "How come the barber is here? I did not mention anyone in particular."

The Emperor asked the guard, "Tell me, was it your idea to call the barber or did someone help you?"

"Your Majesty, it was Birbal's suggestion," said the guard.

Once again Akbar was impressed with Birbal's wisdom.

Management Moral: *Some problems have obvious solutions if you know where to look for them. Presence of mind and observation can go a long way in getting you out of a tricky situation, which at first sight seems insurmountable. The ultimate synthesiser is of course an analytical, sharp and logical mind. The guards observed the Emperor running his fingers through his stubble but it was Birbal's logical mind which registered that the Emperor's request – "call him at once" – could be connected to what the Emperor was doing when he gave that order.*

■ ■ ■

34. Fear is the Key

Problem

One day in Court, Akbar told Birbal, "Birbal my people are basically obedient. I have taught them the right values."

Birbal smiled and said, "Your Majesty, it's true by far that your people are obedient. But this virtue has also to do with fear. They fear you too."

Now Akbar thought of himself as benevolent; the thought of his people fearing him did not appeal to him. Birbal agreed to prove his statement.

Birbal's Solution

Following Birbal's instructions Akbar announced in Court, "I will be going on a hunting trip for a couple of days. In my absence all courtiers must pour a pot of milk in the tub in the courtyard at night."

The tub was placed in the courtyard and Akbar left for his outing.

Certain that his orders would be followed, next morning Akbar returned with Birbal. He went to the courtyard to examine the tub and found that it was full of water.

Akbar was dumbfounded, he could not believe his eyes, but the fact was that the tub was full of water instead of milk.

Akbar looked at Birbal and the latter said, "Your Majesty, we have to complete the experiment. Today ask them to repeat the task and let it be known that you will personally check the contents."

The royal command went and once more the tub was placed in the courtyard. There was a long queue of courtiers to pour their pot of milk into the tub.

Next morning when Akbar went with Birbal to examine the tub, he found that it was overflowing with milk.

Akbar asked Birbal to explain this. Birbal said, "O Sire! The first day each one of your courtiers thought that since there was no one to check, they could get away with pouring water in the tub instead of milk. But on the second day when it was known that you yourself would check, they obeyed you."

Akbar realised that fear plays a great role in obedience.

Management Moral: *We should check our facts before jumping to conclusions that are convenient, attractive or soothing to our egos.*

Since it is an accepted fact that fear always plays a part in obedience of authority, the authority in question will benefit from this knowledge. For if those in authority are not aware of this fact and become pally with subordinates, the latter lose their fear and the former lose their authority.

■ ■ ■

35. Four Fools

Problem

One evening while Akbar and Birbal were taking a walk, Akbar said, "Birbal I have heard that there are many fools in my kingdom, but so far I haven't seen any, so today we shall search for four fools."

As they were walking they came across a man riding a horse. He was carrying a bundle of wood on his head!

Birbal was surprised to see this. "Hey! You are riding a horse, but why are you carrying a load on your head?"

The man replied, "Sir, this horse is very precious to me. He is already carrying my weight. So I am carrying this load of wood on my head. If I put it on him it will be difficult for him to carry more weight!"

Birbal looked at Akbar and said, "Your Highness, we have just met the first fool."

Akbar agreed, "Now we need to look for three other fools."

As they were strolling, it grew dark, and they started walking back to the palace. On the way they saw a man searching for something.

Birbal asked the man, "What are you looking for?"

"I am searching for a coin that I lost here yesterday," replied the man.

"But why are you looking for it today?" asked Birbal.

"I was very tired yesterday, so I have come to look for it today," replied the man.

"Did you lose the coin at this spot where you are searching?" asked Birbal.

"No Sir, not here. I lost it on the other side of the road," said the man.

"But if you lost it on the other side of the road, why are you searching for it here?" asked Akbar, totally amazed.

"That's because it is dark on that side, Sire. I cannot see anything there. Since there is a street lamp here, it is easier to search here," said the man.

Akbar was amused. "Your Majesty! That is the second fool," said Birbal.

They came back to the palace and Akbar said, "Birbal, we still haven't accomplished our task. We need to look for two more fools tomorrow."

"Your Majesty! Our task is accomplished. We have found all the four fools."

"How is that?" asked the Emperor.

Birbal's Solution

"Two fools are present right here," said Birbal.

"Here? What do you mean? Who are the fools here?" asked Akbar.

"Your Majesty, for no reason at all I spent my valuable time looking for fools. Doesn't that make me a fool, too?" said Birbal.

"And who is the fourth one?" asked Akbar.

"Pardon me Sire, but you know, for no reason at all you accompanied me in looking for the fools. So you can guess who the fourth fool is!" smiled Birbal.

Akbar was greatly amused. In his search for fools, he had proved himself to be a fool.

Management Moral: *Never underestimate anyone's capacity for foolishness – including your own!*

Birbal was doubly wise though he called himself foolish. He resorted to an old trick which many mothers use to fool their little ones. By ridiculing their own behaviour and terming it silly, Birbal managed to stop the Emperor from continuing to indulge in a useless, foolish and futile exercise.

■ ■ ■

36. The Glutton

Problem

Akbar had a real passion for food. In his royal kitchen were employed all kinds of master chefs, who made a variety of gourmet dishes. Often Akbar would throw a banquet for his courtiers to enjoy these meals in the palace gardens. The star of the show, of course, would be Akbar's wise and witty minister, Birbal.

Once at one such banquet Birbal was seated next to Emperor Akbar. After the meal, bowls of pistachios were served to all. Both Birbal and Akbar went on eating the pistachios and they threw the shells under their chairs.

Soon there were heaps of pistachio shells under their chairs. Akbar saw the heaps and thought of playing a trick on Birbal. He thought to himself, "For once let me outwit the clever Birbal."

Quietly, Akbar pushed his heap of shells under Birbal's chair with his foot. Birbal did not notice him do this. All of a sudden Akbar sprang from his chair and with a bewildered look he said aloud, "I don't believe this Birbal! How could you eat so many pistachios? You really are a glutton!"

Birbal's Solution

All the courtiers heard this and looked at the big heap of pistachio shells under Birbal's chair. But Birbal was unperturbed; he knew that Akbar had played a trick on him. But the clever Birbal could not allow the Emperor and the courtiers to ridicule him.

Promptly, he said to Akbar, "Your Majesty, you are absolutely right. I am a glutton. It is true that I have eaten a lot of pistachios. But Your Majesty, you really surprise me! How could you eat the pistachios along with the shells?"

Birbal requested the courtiers to look under Akbar's chair. They did not see a single shell there and neither were there any shells in his bowl. The courtiers burst out laughing.

Akbar turned red in the face. He had attempted to trick Birbal and in the end himself became the butt of ridicule!

Although truly embarrassed, he greatly appreciated Birbal's wit and humour.

Management Moral: *Repartee is often a way out of unpleasant situations.*

But if you can't take a joke yourself in good spirit, you may as well refrain from joking about others. The ability and willingness to joke with each other improves our sense of humour and brings people closer. The closer you are, within limits obviously, the better you work together. Besides, humour relieves the monotony and tedium of routine work and adds spice to life.

However, the story also illustrates that if you really want to show off your wit at a party by outwitting someone, don't choose the wisest and wittiest person around or the joke will turn on you and your efforts will be wasted.

■ ■ ■

37. The Golden Gallows

Problem

One day Akbar came to Court in a very bad mood. Unlike his true self, that day he snapped at several courtiers. The courtiers were apprehensive and sat quietly, till the Emperor left the Court.

Later when Birbal met Akbar in private, he asked him the reason for his anger. "Oh Birbal, do not ask! It is my son-in-law. The scoundrel is really annoying," Akbar was furious once again.

Birbal tried to calm him down, "Your Majesty, if you tell me what has happened, may be we could find a solution to the problem."

"Birbal, it has been a year since I saw my daughter. My son-in-law does not send her here to see us," complained Akbar.

"That is not such a big problem. I will send somebody right away to bring Your Majesty's daughter here," assured Birbal.

"You think I haven't already done that? My son-in-law is a stubborn man! He refuses to send my daughter to me. I simply detest such sons-in-law. Now there is something you must do for me, Birbal. Please arrange to put up gallows in the open grounds of the city. I will send all the sons-in-law in my kingdom to the gallows," announced Akbar, seething with rage.

Birbal couldn't believe his ears. How could the Emperor go to this extreme! He tried to pacify Akbar, but to no avail.

For the first time the situation was truly out of his hands. Birbal couldn't think of anything to stop Akbar. So he went to the city grounds and made arrangements for the gallows.

Birbal's Solution

After a week the gallows were ready and Birbal took Akbar on an inspection tour. Akbar was quite pleased, "And now I can eliminate all the sons-in-law in my kingdom. What a relief!"

After a while, Akbar noticed a set of golden and silver gallows. "Birbal, may I ask for whom those special gallows are meant for?"

Birbal replied plainly, "The golden gallows are for you, Your Majesty. And the silver one is for me."

Bewildered, Akbar said, "I didn't ask you to do any such thing. Why should we go to the gallows?"

Birbal replied, "Your Majesty, you wish to send all the sons-in-law in this kingdom to the gallows. Both of us are also the sons-in-law of somebody. How can we exclude ourselves? Since you are the Emperor I arranged for a grand golden gallows for you. The silver one is for me, your Wazir. Don't you think it is appropriate?"

Akbar was amused and impressed by Birbal's wisdom. "What would I ever do without you Birbal," so saying he laughed. He realised his mistake and revoked the order.

Management Moral: *When you categorise people in haste and anger, make sure you don't fall into the same category. If we put ourselves in the shoes of the people under us on whom we pass judgement, we would usually want to review our judgement and rephrase it. The result of generalising the judgement we pass on one person, as applicable to a whole class of people, can be very damaging. In order to always be just, vividly imagine yourself in the shoes of your victim.*

■ ■ ■

38. Hussain Khan's Aspirations

Problem

Akbar greatly favoured his wise and witty minister, Birbal. The other courtiers were jealous of Birbal and often plotted to get rid of him. On one occasion they plotted to use Hussain Khan, the Emperor's brother-in-law, to achieve their goal.

In a private meeting with Hussain Khan, the conniving courtiers suggested, "Hussain Khan, as the Emperor's brother-in-law, you should be the chief minister instead of Birbal."

"But the Emperor does not feel so," said Hussain Khan.

"Why don't you ask your sister to plead your case with the Emperor?" said the cunning courtiers.

"That's a brilliant idea! Why didn't I think of it before?"

Hussain Khan was excited. He approached his sister, the Queen, to put forth his case.

"I will try to persuade the Emperor," promised his sister.

A few days later Akbar was visiting the Queen's chamber. "What's the matter? You seem upset, Begum. Is anything bothering you?" asked Akbar. "Is there anything I can do?"

"Yes! I want you to make my brother, Hussain Khan, the chief minister at your Court, in place of Birbal," said the Queen.

Akbar was astounded. "How can I do that? A chief minister has to be intelligent to run the affairs of this vast empire. Your brother cannot handle this job. Also, I cannot get rid of Birbal, unless I have a reason."

"Well then you can give him an impossible task to perform. If he fails you have to get rid of him," said the angry Queen.

"Alright, you suggest the task," said Akbar.

"When you are in the palace garden tomorrow, insist that Birbal should bring me to you. He will not succeed come what may," said the Queen. She was sure that this time Birbal would fail.

The next day, when Akbar was in the garden, Birbal approached him. "Jahanpanah, you seem worried. What is the matter?"

"It's the Begum, she is upset with me. It's breaking my heart. Can you bring her to me this minute. I know only you can do it," said Akbar. "But if you fail you will have to lose your post to Hussain Khan. I am sure it will please my Begum." So saying Akbar started pacing up and down.

"Your wish is my command, Jahanpanah." After bowing to Akbar, Birbal headed for the Queen's chamber. He knew the plan was hatched by the jealous courtiers.

Birbal's Solution

Later in the Queen's chamber, Birbal said, "Your Majesty, I come with a message from the Emperor. He is in the palace garden and he wants you to…"

Just then a messenger came in. "What is it?" asked Birbal.

"Sir, the message is only for your ears," said the messenger.

As the messenger whispered into Birbal's ears, three of his words were distinctly audible,

"Psst… she is… psst… beautiful."

The Queen was all ears. Birbal turned to her and said, "Now the whole situation has changed. You need not come, Your Highness." So saying, Birbal left.

The Queen's curiosity was aroused. She thought to herself, "The messenger was talking about a beautiful maiden. Perhaps the Emperor does not want me to see him with her."

Flushed with anger and curiosity the Queen rushed to the palace garden. She was surprised to see the Emperor alone.

"But Begum, you said you would not come!" said Akbar.

"I have been tricked by Birbal, Your Highness," complained the Queen.

"Did he lie to get you here? If so, I will punish him."

The Queen told him all that had transpired and they had a good laugh. Just then Birbal arrived. "You win again Birbal," said Akbar, once again pleased by Birbal's smart thinking.

Management Moral: *Arousing people's curiosity is a way of getting them to do things they would otherwise be reluctant to undertake. Besides his shrewd intelligence, Birbal obviously was a good psychologist too — he knew just what emotions to arouse in the Queen, for her to rush to the Emperor in spite of her resolve not to go to him; a jealous wife could never resist this curious situation. Learning the psychology of people's behaviour can be of immense help in your career.*

■ ■ ■

39. The Most Precious Thing

Problem

One day Emperor Akbar was furious with his wife. In a fit of rage, he said, "Begum, I never want to see your face again. Please go to your father's house."

The Begum was really upset and frightened. She couldn't understand what to do and so she sought the help of Birbal. After narrating the entire episode, she asked for his advice.

Birbal pacified her. "Do not worry Begum, such quarrels do occur in a family. Just do as I tell you and all will be well."

Birbal's Solution

After hearing Birbal's plan, the Begum went back to the palace to meet Akbar.

"Your Majesty, I thought I would serve you all my life. But if you wish me to leave, I will do just that," said the Begum.

Akbar was once again furious on seeing her. "Say whatever you have to and leave immediately!" he said.

The Begum humbly put forward her proposition, "Your Majesty, since I will not be seeing you for the rest of my life, I wish to invite you to my palace for dinner one last time. Please come tonight. Also, please allow me to take with me my most precious possession, that I may keep as a memory of you."

Akbar consented and the Begum left. That night, Akbar went to the Begum's palace for dinner. She had prepared all his favourite dishes.

At the end of the dinner, she offered him a glass of milk. The Begum had added sleeping pills in the milk. As soon as Akbar finished the glass of milk, he lay on the bed and fell fast asleep. The Begum sent for Birbal.

Birbal arrived with a carriage. Akbar was put into the carriage and sent with the Begum to her father's house.

The next morning when Akbar awoke, he looked around him puzzled. The room seemed unfamiliar. Then he saw the Begum sitting at his bedside, and she said, "Pardon me, my Lord! But you are in my father's house. If you remember, yesterday you had granted me a wish to carry with me my most precious possession. You are, indeed, my most precious possession. So I have brought you along with me."

Akbar was touched by what the Begum had said. He realised his mistake and returned to the palace with the Begum.

Management Moral: *Love can overcome animosity. Peaceful action against unreasonable opposition achieves the best results. An argument with a superior can yield nothing worthwhile, except trouble, while a premeditated, well thought-out and positive response will make a world of difference.*

■ ■ ■

40. The Mother Tongue

Problem

Once a Brahmin visited Akbar's Court. The Brahmin had heard a lot about the wise men who advised Akbar and so, addressing the Court, he said, "I challenge you to find out what my mother tongue is. If you fail to do so, you will have to accept defeat."

The courtiers asked the Brahmin several questions in different languages and the Brahmin replied to them in the language that he was spoken to. He spoke all languages very fluently as if they were his mother tongue. The courtiers could not guess his mother tongue.

At the end of the session the Brahmin told Akbar, "I give you seven days to find out my mother tongue. Is the challenge accepted?"

Birbal's Solution

With Birbal's consent Akbar accepted the challenge. The Brahmin was putting up in an inn in the city. That night when he was fast asleep, Birbal tiptoed into his room. He tickled the Brahmin's ear with a feather. The Brahmin moved a bit in discomfort and went back to sleep. Once again, Birbal tickled his ear. Now the Brahmin was really upset; he got up and shouted angrily in Marathi, "Hey! Who is it? Why are you bothering me?"

He got off his bed and looked around in the dark. Birbal crouched in a corner of the dark room, but the Brahmin didn't notice him. The Brahmin was soon snoring, and Birbal tiptoed out of the room.

On the seventh day the Brahmin appeared in Court. Birbal spoke to the Brahmin in different languages. Finally, he said to Akbar, "Your Majesty, the Brahmin's mother tongue is Marathi."

The Brahmin was astounded. He accepted defeat and left the Court.

"Tell us Birbal, how did you guess the Brahmin's mother tongue?" asked Akbar.

"Very simple, Sire! A man will speak his mother tongue when he is in distress or when he is suddenly woken up from deep slumber."

Much to their amusement, Birbal then told the Court of his clandestine visit to the inn and what transpired there.

Management Moral: *When you want people to tell you the truth, catch them off guard – the truth will be revealed. And there is no point in ever trying to hide any details about your identity from the people around you — who and what you are and where you hail from. Even if you try to hide these facts, the cat will be out of the bag sooner rather than later. It is better to make your personal details known from the beginning of your acquaintance.*

■ ■ ■

41. Most Popular Profession

Problem

One day Akbar resolved to find out which profession was the most popular in his capital. He asked the courtiers; some said trade, others said masonry, but the general consensus was on soldiering.

Birbal's Solution

When Birbal's turn came, he arose from his seat, bowed before Akbar and said, "Your Majesty, in my opinion the most popular profession is medicine." This was surprising as one could count the number of physicians in the city. The court physician was furious and said that Birbal had no clue about how difficult it was to train in this profession and advise people on medical problems. Birbal smiled and said, "I can prove my statement, Your Majesty, if you come with me tomorrow morning."

Akbar agreed, and the next morning met Birbal on a major crossroad in the city.

Birbal had a bandage on one hand. Akbar looked at it and asked what the matter was. Birbal said, "I cut my hand while chopping fruits for breakfast. Please, Your Majesty, you will have to write down the names of all the physicians we come across."

"I will do that Birbal, but be sure to wash that wound well and apply some ointment on it," said Akbar.

"I will, Your Majesty, but only after I have proven my statement," said Birbal.

They sat at the busy crossroad all through the day. Birbal was a well-known personality, so everyone who passed by asked Birbal about his injury and advised him about some medication or the other. As the day wore on, the list grew long and by afternoon Akbar was tired of writing names, so he suggested they go home.

Birbal asked for the list and said, "My Lord, you forgot to write your own name at the top of the list. You were the first one to advise me!"

Management Moral: *Unsought advice is cheap. And the treatment it gets from the person you give it to will be cheap, too. It is best to refrain from showering a lot of advice on matters that you are not qualified to handle. And from your side, make sure you check the credentials of those who counsel you, both in personal and professional life.*

So also, when you do wish to give advice, stick to areas in which you specialise and make your credentials known.

■ ■ ■

42. Sleepless Nights

Problem

Akbar spent many sleepless nights worrying about his kingdom and the subjects. Gradually, this started to tell on his health. Although he was examined by many physicians, none could cure him of his sleeplessness.

Then one day, he was examined by a physician from Persia. The physician said, "My Lord, there is only one cure for this disease. Every night before you sleep, you must listen to a story. This will rid you of all your worries and you will sleep peacefully."

"But who will tell me bedtime stories?" Akbar mused.

"Do not worry, Your Majesty! Every night one of your courtiers will come to your chamber to tell you a story," suggested Birbal.

"Hmm, that sounds great, Birbal!" agreed Akbar. So the royal command was sent out and every night a courtier would visit Akbar's chamber to tell him a story.

But this didn't quite work. The courtier would be tired of telling a story and Akbar would not fall asleep. He was always anxious and would repeatedly say, "What then?" "What then?".

Finally, the courtier would be so fed up and tired that he himself would fall asleep, while Akbar remained wide awake!

Birbal's Solution

Then came the day when it was Birbal's turn to tell a tale. Birbal began his story thus: "Once upon a time in a forest…"

"What then?" asked Akbar.

"There was a little cottage in which lived a farmer with his large family."

"What then?" asked Akbar.

"The farmer ploughed the fields and grew crops. After harvesting the crops, he stored the grains in his cottage."

"What then?"

"But the farmer was faced with a problem. Birds would enter his cottage and pick his grains."

"What then?" Akbar couldn't quite relax. By then, Birbal was furious and he thought something had to be done about Akbar's "What then?" question.

Birbal continued the story: "The farmer decided to tackle the bird problem."

"What then?"

"The farmer put the grains in a big pot and sealed the mouth of the pot with a thick cloth."

"What then?"

"The birds came into the cottage and couldn't get the grains."

"What then?"

"The birds spotted a mouse in the cottage. They talked the mouse into gnawing the cloth on the pot."

"What then?"

"Having found the grains, the birds came in one by one. There were a thousand birds. The first bird entered the cottage, picked a grain, flapped its wings and flew away."

"What then?"

"The second bird came, picked a grain, flapped its wings and flew away."

"What then?"

"The third bird came, picked a grain, flapped its wings and flew away."

"What then?"

"The fourth bird came, picked a grain, flapped its wings and flew away."

By now Akbar was completely bored. He asked Birbal, "How many birds still to go?"

Birbal smiled, "Your Majesty, only four have flown so far. It will take quite a while for a thousand birds to fly away."

Akbar yawned and said, "Birbal, can the rest of the birds fly tomorrow? I am very sleepy now."

Within minutes he was asleep and Birbal left his chamber.

Next morning, Akbar was really bright and cheerful, "Birbal, I really enjoyed your story and got a real good night's sleep."

"What then?" asked Birbal.

"The next bird came, picked a grain, flapped its wings and flew away!" replied Akbar.

And both laughed merrily.

Management Moral: *Some people don't realise what they are doing until you mirror their behaviour. So rather than have an argument or find fault with their behaviour, which would not convince them that their behaviour is ridiculous, some mimicry does the trick. Especially if it is not very blatant but rather subtle like Birbal's, it may be appropriate to even make your superior realise the oddities in his behaviour.*

■ ■ ■

43. The Witness

Problem

In the reign of the great Emperor Akbar, a Brahmin once came to see the city of Delhi. The Brahmin had no one in Delhi and a merchant took pity on him and offered shelter.

The merchant gave him some food and allowed him to spend the night in a room in his house.

In those days, Delhi was infested with thieves. For the safety of his subjects, Akbar had instructed his guards to patrol the streets by night. However, one of the guards himself was a thief. He robbed people while on duty, and so far had managed to get away with it.

That night the guard came to the house of the merchant who had given shelter to the Brahmin. The guard made a hole in the wall and entered the room in which the Brahmin was asleep. In the room was a locked box that belonged to the merchant. The guard took the box and stealthily tried to get away. The Brahmin, however, was awakened by the guard's footsteps. The guard made a dash for the hole in the wall, but the Brahmin grabbed him.

The guard pleaded with the Brahmin, "Please let me go. We can share all that is in this box. You will be rich!"

The Brahmin was outraged, "I will never do that; let me call the merchant."

But before he could call the merchant, the guard started yelling. The merchant was awakened by all the commotion and rushed to the guest room. Before the Brahmin could say anything, the guard said excitedly, "Sir, this man was trying to run away with your box. I caught him just in time. Look, he has broken your wall here."

The merchant was outraged. Turning to the Brahmin he said, "How could you do this to me? That too, after I gave you food and shelter. You have betrayed my trust."

The merchant believed the guard, and took the matter to court. The guard, the Brahmin and the merchant were produced before Birbal.

Birbal's Solution

Birbal called one of his trusted men and whispered something in his ear and the man left the Court. He then called the guard and the Brahmin and began questioning them.

A little while later, the man who had left the Court earlier came running back. He was very flustered and said to Birbal, "Sir, I was visiting the temple with my son. On the way out my son fell down and became unconscious. I have to rush him to a doctor. Please send two of your men to help me carry him."

Birbal said, "I need you here for some important work, please wait here. I will send this guard and the Brahmin to the temple. They will bring your son here. Do not worry."

The Brahmin and the guard reached the temple. They picked up the unconscious boy and headed back for the Court. On the way back, the Brahmin said to the guard, "Why did you get me into trouble? You broke into the merchant's house, stole his box and were running away. But when I caught you, you lied to everyone and have now made me look like the culprit. Why did you do this?"

The guard replied, "I had to do that to save my skin. Too bad you didn't accept my offer to share the stolen goods. That way we would both have become rich! Now you will have to bear the consequences. Ha! Ha! That's the price of your foolishness!"

The Brahmin and the guard continued to argue as they carried the boy back to the Court. On reaching the Court, they laid the boy down on the floor.

Once again, Birbal urged the suspects to tell the truth.

But each accused the other of the theft. Birbal was truly irritated, "How are we ever going to get the culprit if the two of you keep arguing."

No sooner did he say this, the 'unconscious' boy arose and said to Birbal, "Sir, the culprit is the guard; he has trapped the poor Brahmin."

The boy narrated all that had transpired between the Brahmin and the guard, while they carried the boy back to the Court. So the wise Birbal acquitted the Brahmin honourably, and sent the guard to jail.

Management Moral: *There are many ways to catch people off guard and get them to tell the truth. One of the ways is what Birbal got the courtier's son to do, as he himself could not pretend he was asleep or unconscious and eavesdrop on the conversation of the guard and the Brahmin.*

This may not be practical in the office, but even if you pretend you are very busy, you may be able to hear many bits of conversation not meant for your ears! This will help you get to the truth of matters at your place of work. Regular informers amongst junior managers can also do a great job in helping you keep in touch with ground realities.

■ ■ ■

44. Constipation

Problem

At one point, Akbar was being given a tough time by Maharana Pratap Singh's valiant army and Akbar was unable to do anything about it. To take out his frustration on Maharana Pratap, he hung a portrait of the latter in his toilet.

Birbal was passing by when he happened to see the picture. Shocked at Akbar for this mean act, he thought of teaching him a lesson.

Birbal's Solution

When Akbar was resting, Birbal suddenly came in and held Akbar's hand to feel his pulse...

He asked, "Your Majesty, how are you now?"

Akbar said, "What has happened to me?"

Birbal replied, "After seeing Maharana Pratap's portrait in your toilet, I thought you were probably suffering from constipation and seeing his picture helped in clearing your bowels!"

The Badshah was totally bowled over and removed the portrait.

Management Moral: *Shock tactics sometimes work. We cover up our own shortcomings by denigrating others. If Akbar had succeeded in defeating Maharana Pratap, he would not have given his portrait demeaning treatment. And if he had channelled his anger to defeat* *him rather than to degrade him, he might have succeeded in defeating him. Hate-based behaviour or writing hate mail does us no good. The same energy could be channelled to change the things we find wrong.*

■ ■ ■

45. Birbal's Explanation

Problem

The Emperor once saw a woman hugging and kissing a child that did not look particularly appealing. The Emperor expressed surprise that a woman could lavish so much love on such an unattractive child.

"That's because it's her own child," explained Birbal. "To a mother her child is always beautiful."

But the Emperor was not satisfied by the explanation.

Birbal's Solution

The next day, Birbal called a guard and in the Emperor's presence ordered him to bring the most beautiful child to the palace.

The following day the guard came to the palace with a small boy with buck teeth and hair that stood up like porcupine quills and hesitantly pushed him in front of the Emperor.

"T-The most beautiful child, Your Majesty," he stammered.

"How do you know he's beautiful?" asked the Emperor.

"My wife, his mother, says so," replied the soldier.

Management Moral: *There is no arguing with a mother's love. It is consistent and unshakeable; nothing can suppress it — neither the child's looks nor others' opinion about the child. There is much to learn from this exemplary love — if we could be half as consistent* *in our relationships, our dealings with our dear ones, colleagues and friends would be much more steady and save everyone a lot of heartache. This story teaches us that everybody is special in some way or the other, though we may not always be able to perceive what it is that makes each person special and loveable.*

■ ■ ■

46. Tracking Down

Problem

Birbal was missing. He and the Emperor had quarrelled and Birbal had stormed out of the palace vowing never to return. Now Akbar missed him and wanted him back but no one knew where he was.

Then the Emperor had a brainwave. He offered a reward of 1,000 gold coins to any man who could come to the palace whilst observing the following condition: the man had to walk in the sun without an umbrella but he had to be in the shade at the same time.

"Impossible," said the people.

Birbal's Solution

Then a villager came carrying a string cot over his head and claimed the prize.

"I've walked in the sun, but at the same time I was in the shade of the strings of the cot!" he said.

It was a brilliant solution. On being questioned, the villager confessed that the idea was suggested by a man living with him.

"It could only be Birbal!" said the Emperor, delighted. Sure enough, it was Birbal and he and the Emperor had a joyous reunion.

Management Moral: *It is not difficult to uncover a talented man if you offer him the right challenge. Many people have talents that lie dormant for lack of challenge and opportunity. As a superior you can make good use of the talents of those under you, whilst giving them the satisfaction and the benefits of their gifts, if you only know how to draw them out.*

■ ■ ■

47. Flowers for the Emperor

Problem

Emperor Akbar and some of his courtiers were strolling through the royal gardens.

"How beautiful!" said the Court poet, drawing the Emperor's attention to a flower growing on a bush. "Man could never produce anything as beautiful."

"Man can sometimes produce more beautiful things," said Birbal.

"I don't believe it!" said the Emperor. "You are talking nonsense, Birbal!"

Birbal's Solution

A few days later Birbal led a master craftsman of Agra into Akbar's presence. The man presented the Emperor with an exquisite marble carving of a bouquet of flowers. The Emperor rewarded him with a thousand gold coins.

Just then a small boy entered and gave Akbar a bunch of roses. Akbar thanked the boy and gave him a silver coin.

"So the carving was more beautiful than the real thing," said Birbal softly and the Emperor realised with a start that once again he had played into the hands of his shrewd courtier.

Management Moral: *A work of art is priceless. It is more beautiful than the real thing insofar as it immortalises reality. If there is a drought in the country there may be no flowers and landscapes with greenery but works of artists will help us liven up our lives. So artistic talent is to be encouraged and we should do our best to support and contribute our mite by patronising talent. We may be able to produce gardens and orchards but we cannot produce an artist. We must make the best of our gifts and the gifted people that we have.*

■ ■ ■

48. Never at a Loss

Problem

Birbal could always give satisfactory replies to the questions of the Emperor. Seeing how much the Emperor relied on Birbal, other ministers and dignitaries in the Court envied Birbal.

The Commander-in-Chief of the army, who was one of this group, seized the opportunity of Birbal's absence from the durbar hall one day to tell the Emperor: "Your Majesty, here there are so many of us with considerable experience. Please consult us also. Why do you always ask Birbal about everything?"

On another day, Akbar came to the audience hall and inquired about Birbal. The Commander-in-Chief said Birbal was away and informed the Emperor that he was ready to answer the Emperor's questions. All others also got up and said they were prepared to do so.

Akbar rose and put the first question to the assembled dignitaries. He warned them that their answer should satisfy him. The first question he put was: *In this world, which is the best flower?*

The Commander-in-Chief replied that the rose was the best flower.

Other ministers mentioned the names of jasmine, champa and other flowers.

The Emperor was not satisfied.

He then fielded a second question: *Which milk is the best milk?*

Once again, there were a variety of answers, none of which satisfied the Emperor.

He then put the third question: *What is the sweetest thing in the world?*

Many replied: Jaggery. One said honey. As before, there were varied replies.

The Emperor then came to the fourth question: *Which leaf ranks highest among leaves?*

The assembled men gave different answers. Akbar was not impressed.

Birbal's Solution

By this time, Birbal had entered the hall. Akbar then put the four questions to him.

Which is the best flower in the world?

Birbal: "The flower of the cotton plant is the best. From the cotton flower, we have cotton, out of which yarn is made and clothes are woven. The cotton flower is therefore of lasting use to mankind. Other flowers are only of temporary value and useless when their fragrance vanishes."

Which is the best milk in the world?

Birbal: "A mother's breast milk is the best, because it nourishes the child."

What is the sweetest thing in the world?

Birbal: "Sweet speech. Through sweet words you can transform any person and give great joy. Men throw stones when a crow caws. But they listen raptly to the sweet call of the cuckoo. Sweetness in speech is sweeter than anything else."

Which is the best leaf in the world?

Birbal: "The betel leaf is the best, Your Majesty. Betel leaves are offered on all auspicious occasions like weddings. The betel leaf is considered sacred and auspicious. Other leaves such as plantain leaves have no special value at all."

Everyone in the audience was amazed at Birbal's intelligent replies, which pleased the Emperor.

Akbar told the gathering that none of their answers had satisfied him, but expressed his appreciation for Birbal's replies. The courtiers realised why the Emperor valued the words of Birbal so much.

Management Moral 1: *Usefulness is the key in everything. Cultivate a ready wit and serve it with common sense; they are appreciated anywhere and can come in handy in difficult situations. This is one of the keys that can lead you to become almost indispensable to your superiors.*

Management Moral 2: *Jealousy does not serve any purpose. Instead of indulging in envy, if the same energy is channelled to improve your knowledge through reading and attending courses relevant to your carrier, you are bound to excel in your department and be able to compete with the best. In such a situation there will be no place for jealousy. On the contrary, you can set an example and encourage others to follow your lead instead of envying you.*

■ ■ ■

49. Becoming a Brahmin...

Problem

Birbal the Brahmin was so wise that Emperor Akbar decided to become a Brahmin, too. Birbal tried to convince him that it was enough to be a good man, but Akbar insisted and demanded a ceremony.

Birbal's Solution

Claiming he was taking him to a holy man who could turn the Moghul Emperor into a Hindu Brahmin, Birbal escorted Akbar along a river where they found a man scrubbing a donkey.

The man explained, "I am changing my donkey into a horse. A holy man said that if I stood by a river and scrubbed my donkey, it would turn into a horse."

Akbar laughed at the fool. "It won't work. It can't work." When Birbal laughed, Akbar realised he had been tricked.

Management Moral: *There is no point in trying to change the unchangeable. Try to improve the changeable and learn to tell the difference. You may be endowed with wisdom and other good qualities naturally or you may acquire them with learning. Whatever the case, it will have nothing to do with your religion, caste, race or colour. Likewise, appreciate a wise person for what he is, irrespective of all the other criteria.*

■ ■ ■

50. Name Chanting

Problem

Apart from his sharp intellect, Birbal was also a devotee of Sri Rama. Wherever Akbar went, he used to take Birbal along with him. During one such instance, when they travelled for some official purpose, they had to take a route through a dense forest. In the course of the journey, both were totally exhausted and famished. So they decided to rest under the shade of a tree for a while before continuing their journey.

Since Akbar was very hungry, he wanted to look around the place to see if he could find a house to get some food. He induced Birbal to follow suit. But Birbal, who was in the midst of Rama Nama Japam (repetition of Rama's Name), asked to be excused.

Akbar looked at Birbal. "Mere chanting of the names of the Lord will not fetch you food. You have to put in your own efforts... You cannot achieve anything otherwise," he said.

So saying, Akbar left Birbal and went off in pursuit of satiating his belly. In a little while he spotted a house. The inmates of the house were overjoyed to see the Emperor coming to their very doorstep for food. They treated him to the best of their capacity. Akbar finished his meal and took a little food for Birbal too.

He met Birbal and gave him the food. "See Birbal, I told you... I made some effort to find food and I got it. You were just sitting and chanting Rama Nama, and you did not get any food."

Birbal's Solution

Birbal ignored the Emperor's scoffing and partook of the food given to him by Akbar.

After he finished the meal, he looked up at Akbar and said, "I have just now experienced the power of Rama Nama, like never before. You are the ruler of the land. But today even the Emperor had to beg for food. And look at me. I was just chanting Rama Nama here and the Rama Nama made the Emperor himself get me food, that too by begging. So I got the food just by sitting here and chanting Rama Nama without any other special efforts. Such is the power of Rama Nama!"

Management Moral: *You have a variety of means available to achieve your goals. It is up to you to select the one most appropriate for the occasion, the most suitable for your temperament and above all most likely to yield results. And if you find that prayer will meet your needs, certainly use it.*

■ ■ ■

51. Wives' Power

Problem

Once Akbar and Birbal were going around in civilian dress. They found that a woman considerably shorter than her husband was slapping him.

Akbar enquired from Birbal why the husband was not retaliating. Birbal said: "Because he is attached to the wife."

Akbar refused to believe this. To check how many of his married citizens listened to their wives, all husbands were asked to assemble in a field.

Then Birbal said: "His Majesty wants to know how many of you follow your wives' decisions. All those who listen to their wives move to the other side."

There was a great exodus of people to the other side. In fact, all moved except one.

Akbar was relieved: "There is at least one who doesn't listen to his wife."

Birbal then asked the man why he didn't move.

The man replied, "Because my wife told me not to go with the crowd!"

Akbar was still not convinced. He said: "There must be a few men who are not dominated by their wives. I will give you two beautiful horses. You go around, and take a few hens also with you. If you find a man who is henpecked, present him with a hen. If you find a man who is not henpecked, then give him a choice: he can either have the black horse or the white horse. These are the most beautiful horses I have, the most costly."

Birbal's Solution

Birbal went around Delhi, and wherever he went he had to present a hen. Only in one place he met a very muscular man – with a strong, muscular body the likes of which he had never seen before — who was sitting in the sun, having his muscles massaged.

Birbal asked him, "Are you a henpecked husband?"

He simply showed his muscles to Birbal and said, "Just hold my hand and I will show you!" He crushed Birbal's hand till Birbal screamed, then he said, "Now, do you have to ask me again? Then I will hit you! The very question is insulting! Who can dominate me?"

A short woman was cooking food inside.

Birbal asked, "Where is your wife?"

He said, "That is my wife cooking inside. You can look at her and then at me, and decide who is the master."

It was so absolutely clear that Birbal said, "Certainly, you are the master, so I will have to take back my accusation. You can choose as a gift from the Emperor either of the horses, black or white."

At this, the man looked at the woman and asked, "Which horse should I choose, black or white?"

And the woman said, "Let it be white!"

Then Birbal said, "Now you get a hen! You may have muscular power, but that does not prove anything."

Management Moral: *There are many kinds of power, some more obvious than others. The power to influence others has nothing to do with the size of the person or his physical strength. Besides, having power and using it are two different things.*

Emotional attachment may dictate how much you want to control the other person and how much you give in to other people trying to control you.

■ ■ ■

52. Lost Respect

Problem

Once, Akbar was presented with a bottle of perfume. While applying it, a drop fell on the floor. He instinctively bent down and rubbed the spot with his fingers. Suddenly, he noticed that Birbal had seen him do so and, therefore, Akbar announced in his Durbar, "Let the fountains be filled with perfume for six days."

Akbar noticed that Birbal was not impressed and he insisted that Birbal tell him the reason.

Birbal's Solution

Birbal replied: "Respect gone with a drop cannot be replaced by filling tanks."

Management Moral 1: *Birbal said it all – lost respect is irreplaceable. If you want to be respected always and want to maintain your dignity and image, see that your behaviour is always in step with the image you want to cultivate. A slip in conduct can erode your credibility forever.*

Management Moral 2: *Too much emphasis on appearances is partly an expression of the hypocrisy within us. Try to balance your need to maintain an outward image of yourself with the reality of what you are.*

■ ■ ■

53. Conquest of the Mind

Problem

Akbar was passing through a spell of melancholy and depression. Nobody could find out the cause of this aberration in the Emperor who was otherwise always full of zest and cheer.

His empire was prosperous and safe from enemies, both internal and external. The subjects, irrespective of caste and creed, loved him. Why then was he in such a depressed frame of mind?

The cause of his melancholy was at last detected. It was the food he ate every day. Of course, he himself had laid down the menu. Neither the cook nor the superintendent of the Imperial kitchen could be blamed. The Emperor had developed abhorrence for meat and a strong aversion to all food. The loss of this important pleasure was weighing heavily on his mind.

So Akbar called Birbal into his presence and commanded that the menu be changed. The command was obeyed. Birbal racked his brains for a long time and discovered from the cook that brinjals had not been served for a long time. He decided on brinjals for a change. He procured baskets full of brinjals, fresh and fine. He got chutney, salad, soup, cutlets and sweet and savoury dishes all prepared from brinjals.

Akbar relished every item and praised Birbal to the skies. It was now brinjal breakfast, brinjal lunch, brinjal dinner. Thus it went on for a few days.

Then Akbar grew disgusted with brinjals, too. He poured all his wrath on Birbal.

Birbal's Solution

Birbal had to switch on to something else. But he knew that something else would also soon prove disgusting to Akbar.

So he went to Akbar and told him boldly: "My Lord, the fault is not in the menu. It is in your own mind, which has fast-changing likes and dislikes. Change your menu everyday and eat everything with the same relish. Once you tune your mind like this and become its master, you will never have this trouble again."

Management Moral 1: *Of all the victories, the conquest of the mind is the most difficult one. But it is also the giver of the greatest power, peace and joy. It can serve as the key to a balanced attitude to life in all its multifarious aspects.*

Management Moral 2: *Variety is the spice of life. If you try to avoid an excessively routine daily schedule, whether in work or in food and entertainment, it will help you keep yourself more interested in these activities of daily life and this, in turn, will help you in avoiding boredom. A high degree of interest leads to better performance, too.*

■ ■ ■

54. Corruption

Problem

The great Emperor Akbar was well aware of the adage, "Power corrupts, and absolute power corrupts absolutely." After hearing a particularly nasty story about a corrupt courtier, the Emperor made an observation to this effect to his celebrated counsel, Birbal.

Birbal disagreed. "Corrupt officials do not need any power to be corrupt," he maintained. "They can invent power."

Birbal's Solution

Like before, Birbal was called upon to prove his assertion. He then went to the bank of the Yamuna River with a bunch of bamboo sticks and some lengths of ordinary string. He stuck a couple of sticks into the ground at various points and made it look as if he was busy taking some critical measurements.

A curious crowd gathered and began inquiring about what was going on. Birbal said nothing. People presumed that he must be busy with some work of the state and it could only mean trouble for the neighbouring area and the community. Without being asked, those in the neighbourhood started offering purses to Birbal, with a vague request to protect them. Birbal maintained his silence. People assumed the purses offered were too small to set off the imminent threat and offered increasingly larger purses.

Substantially enriched, Birbal left after some time with his sticks and string and won the wager amount from the Emperor.

Management Moral: *Rather than power, corruption needs cooperation from its victims in order to succeed. Denied cooperation even the most corrupt will collapse. This needs determination and some sacrifice from the victims. If the victims are weak and encourage corruption for quick gain, then the corrupt prosper and flourish. Rather than blame the system which affects all of us, one way to curb corruption would be to ask how each of us is contributing to it, and refrain from getting things done by bribing or soliciting bribes to do our duty.*

■ ■ ■

55. Who Shaves the Barber?

Problem

During the reign of Emperor Akbar it became very fashionable to grow a long beard at the Royal Court in Agra. As there were no safety razors in those days, barbers used to shave the men. However, due to the fashion of long beards, the business of barbers suffered tremendously. Samir was one such enterprising and greedy barber.

It was the custom in those days for the Emperor to distribute gifts to citizens who entered the Court. When Samir entered the Court he was offered a silver coin, which was the standard gift in those days, but he refused it and demanded to see the Emperor. Those were the days when emperors were very concerned about their subjects and a lot more accessible.

Akbar came and asked the barber what the trouble was. The impudent Samir blamed the fashion of beards on the Emperor, who had started the entire trend, and consequently held him responsible for the misfortune of his dwindling business.

The Emperor couldn't do anything but agree, as this was true: he was the one who had started the fashion because he felt it made him look wiser.

Samir asked the Emperor to rectify this injustice to him by making him the sole barber in Agra. As he was feeling somewhat guilty and because it was his birthday, Akbar agreed and issued a firman that: "Henceforth all those and only those who don't shave themselves will have to be shaved by Samir. This firman applies only to citizens of Agra. Anyone who violates this shall be punished with death."

Samir went back a satisfied man and became the only barber (for shaving anyway!) in the city. He discovered that this monopoly gave him the power to keep increasing his prices without fear that there would be any competition to check him. The citizens of the city were now forced to get very expensive shaves.

Eventually the men who didn't shave themselves got tired of having to pay the exorbitant amount that Samir had begun charging. They sent Puroh as their representative to the Emperor but the Emperor could hardly revoke his own firman! So Puroh went to Birbal and told him the entire story.

Birbal's Solution

Birbal read the firman and turned towards Puroh.

Birbal: "When was this firman issued?"

Puroh: "Huzoor, it was issued eight months ago."

Birbal: "And does Samir have a beard?"

Puroh: "Huzoor, I do not think this is the time to discuss fashion. It will be better if you apply your mind to this problem."

Birbal: "You fool, I am doing just that! Now tell me if Samir has a beard."

Puroh: "I last saw him two weeks ago and he didn't have one then, but I cannot say for sure if he does now."

Birbal: "That is good enough. Now go and fetch him. Tell him that the Emperor wishes to see him immediately. I will see you there."

Presently, Puroh got Samir to see the Emperor and found that Birbal was waiting there.

Birbal: "Samir, you have made enough money through your exorbitant rates. It will be best if you agree to the Emperor revoking this firman."

Samir: "Huzoor, it is not really necessary for me to agree. The Emperor has the power to do as he pleases. If he wishes, he can cancel the firman and there is nothing that I can do."

Akbar: "This I will not do unless you consent. I do not take back a gift that I have given and I have given this on my birthday."

Birbal: "Do you agree to this Samir?"

Samir knew when he had a good thing going. But since Birbal was a powerful minister, Samir did not turn him down nor did he agree with him.

Eventually, Birbal got tired of trying to convince Samir.

Birbal: "Just one more thing before you leave Samir. When did you last shave yourself?"

Samir: "Sir, it is my practice to shave every morning."

Birbal: "Do you go to some other barber?"

Samir: "No, Sir. After the firman, I am the only barber in this city. I shave myself."

Birbal: "Your Majesty, in accordance with your firman, Samir should be put to death."

Samir: "Your Majesty, if you are going to put me to death because I did not agree, I do not think that people will ever accept your generosity again."

Akbar: "Have you lost your mind Birbal? I do not like what Samir is doing but I did issue the firman." The Emperor seemed perplexed.

Birbal: "That is true but he himself has violated your firman. Your Majesty, your firman makes it very clear that anyone who doesn't shave himself can get a shave only from Samir."

Akbar: "That is correct."

Birbal: "He can only shave those who don't shave themselves."

Akbar: "That is also correct."

Birbal: "Then he should be put to death. He was not allowed to shave himself!"

Samir was stunned. He turned to the Emperor and said, "Sire, but according to the firman, if I didn't shave myself then I had to shave myself as your firman says that ...*those who don't shave themselves will have to be shaved by Samir.*"

To this Birbal replied, "That is true, but you also cannot shave yourself as you violate the firman which also says that ...*ONLY those who don't shave themselves will have to be shaved by Samir.* And if you shave yourself then you clearly do not qualify to be shaved by yourself. As you have violated this, you will have to be put to death as per the same firman that you have exploited so far."

Samir turned white and beseeched the Emperor, "But Your Majesty, with this firman I violate it no matter what I do. If I shave myself, I violate it and if I don't shave myself, I violate it. No matter what I do I will be put to death."

The Emperor looked at Samir, "You are being punished for your own greed. For the last eight months you have been charging the citizens five times the price that was charged earlier and I could not intervene, as it was my own firman. You did not complain that this was an unjust firman then. But I do not like having to put you to death. Birbal, is there a way out?"

Birbal found a way. He said that since the firman applied only to Agra, Samir should be banished from the city and pardoned for his violation of the law.

Management Moral: *People who succeed through devious means are liable to fall into their own trap. Self-control is one of the basic requisites for a balanced character. Unless your employees are tested for it, you will not know who will be unable to resist the temptation to make a quick buck at your cost only to fall into his own trap and ruin his career.*

■ ■ ■

56. The Source of Wisdom

Problem

Akbar once asked Birbal from where he had acquired all his wisdom.

Birbal's Solution

Birbal said: "From fools. I observe their actions and try not to repeat their mistakes. Thus I get wiser and wiser. There are enough fools and madmen around to provide anyone with wisdom."

Management Moral: *Learning from the mistakes and experience of others is the most efficient and inexpensive way of learning. And repeating one's own mistakes is the most expensive way of learning. There is no lack of opportunity to observe the mistakes of the people you work with. If you try to learn by observing other people's mistakes over and above learning from your own mistakes, you are likely to become doubly wise like Birbal.*

■ ■ ■

57. Harem Scare

Problem

Emperor Akbar once saw a tribal woman deliver her baby in the middle of the forest without any help and resume her journey home carrying a large bundle of firewood. Highly impressed, he ordered that, henceforth, women in his harem would not get any medical aid to deliver babies.

Birbal's Solution

Much alarmed, the royal women appealed to Birbal for help. A couple of weeks later, when Akbar was strolling around in the garden with Birbal, he was shocked to see his precious rose plants had all withered. Naturally, he was furious with the gardener.

Birbal then intervened and said that forests have mighty trees though no one ever bothers to water and nurture them. Why then should roses be pampered?

Akbar got the hint and withdrew his order about abolishing medical attention to the women in his harem.

Management Moral: *Everything needs an appropriate environment to be nurtured to its full potential. Besides, yardsticks for one cannot be applied to others.*

■ ■ ■

58. The Real King

Problem

The King of Egypt had heard about Birbal's wisdom and wanted to test him. So he asked Emperor Akbar to send Birbal to his Court. Birbal left for Egypt the next day.

When Birbal arrived in Egypt, the Chief Minister of Egypt told Birbal, "The King will see you in the morning tomorrow." The following morning Birbal entered the Court and saw five identical kings, all seated on different royal thrones wearing the same royal costumes and jewellery.

Birbal's Solution

Birbal was momentarily perplexed. However, he observed all of them for some time and then walked up to one of them and said, "Long live the King!"

"How did you know I was the real King?"

Birbal replied, "Your Majesty, the other 'kings' were watching you closely and trying to imitate you all the while. On the other hand, you were sitting calm, composed and relaxed. So I guessed you had to be the real King."

The King praised Birbal and rewarded him with rich gifts and jewels.

Management Moral: *Imitations seldom come up to the standards of the original. Disguise and deception are not easy to pull off, more so in the presence of a superior who expects you to be faultless.*

■ ■ ■

59. The Merchant Who Wanted Too Much

Problem

Two prosperous ghee merchants had their shops next to each other. One day one of them decided to borrow 500 gold coins from his colleague and obtained his loan without any hassle. But when it was time to repay his debt, he refused to do so. He would simply not admit he had borrowed the money and said his friend was making up the story.

The merchant who had lent the money went to the Emperor for justice. As usual the case was assigned to Birbal, who summoned both and heard each one's story. Birbal then asked for ten days' time and sent both the merchants away.

Birbal's Solution

After giving the problem deep thought, he ordered ten tins of oil. Each tin contained 10 kg oil and in two of them Birbal put a gold coin. Then he called all the ten oil merchants and gave each of them one of the tins saying, "Examine this oil carefully and determine the price. You may take the tins home but please return them after three days." He gave the two containers with the gold coins to the two merchants whose case was pending.

The merchant who had lent the money was an honest man and as soon as he found the gold coin he returned the coin to Birbal. But his dishonest neighbour found the coin and gave it as pocket money to his son.

On the appointed day all ten merchants returned to give Birbal their decision about the market price of the oil. Birbal carefully examined the tin of the merchant who had been accused of not paying his debt and besides noticing that the gold coin had disappeared, also noticed that the quantity of oil had reduced considerably.

When Birbal inquired about it, the merchant replied, "Sir, it must have reduced while I heated it for testing."

Birbal answered, "Oh, is it? Let me check what you are saying. I'll be back right away." And saying so, he went inside to his servant. But instead of testing the oil, he asked one of the servants to go to the suspect's house and ask his son to return the gold coin his father had found in the tin of oil.

Very soon the boy entered the Court with the gold coin and immediately Birbal asked him, "Did you bring all the five coins that your father found in the oil?"

And the prompt answer was, "There was only one gold coin in the oil can, not five, Sir."

Birbal then addressed the merchant: "You did not prove to be trustworthy with a single gold coin that I dropped in your tin of oil. Besides, you also removed part of the oil and blamed the decrease on the heat testing. Why would you be speaking the truth about 500 gold coins that you owe your neighbour? What do you have to say now?"

The merchant could not find any way to defend himself and was forced to admit his fault in the presence of all the oil traders.

Management Moral: *The truth cannot remain under wraps forever. Dishonesty is discovered sooner or later and when that happens the humiliation falls both on oneself and one's family. Once lost, your reputation amongst business counterparts and clients can seldom be regained.*

■ ■ ■

60. Mother's Love

Problem

Emperor Akbar once told Birbal there was no love greater than a mother's love. Birbal countered this by saying the only love we have is for our self.

Birbal's Solution

To prove it, he placed a baby monkey and its mother in an empty tank and started filling it. The monkey held the baby in its arms as the water rose, then above its head.

When the water level crossed her nose and she was unable to breathe even by jumping, in a desperate attempt at self-preservation, she put the baby monkey under her feet and stood on it....

Management Moral: *Even a mother's love, the greatest love, sometimes has its limits. Similarly, if tested about his faithfulness at the cost of personal survival, the average man will not put his boss before him. That is especially the risk of low wages. A good offer will tempt him to give away information about you or the company that you consider confidential. But if he is able to provide well for himself and his family, he is more likely to remain faithful.*

■ ■ ■

61. What Does God Do?

Problem

Once Akbar asked Birbal, "What does God do?"

Birbal replied, "Sire, even a common shepherd can answer this question."

Birbal's Solution

The Emperor ordered Birbal to bring a shepherd to the Court. The rustic boy was asked the same question, upon which he countered, "Is the Emperor asking this as a teacher or as a pupil?"

The Emperor replied, "As a pupil."

The shepherd countered, "Look at the pupil's insolence. He is sitting on a throne, while the teacher stands on the ground."

Akbar was embarrassed. He descended from the throne, made the boy wear his royal robes and seated him on the throne. Then he wore the shepherd's clothes, stood before him with folded hands and again asked, "Teacher, what does God do?"

The shepherd replied, "God turns a shepherd into an emperor and an emperor into a shepherd."

Management Moral 1: *There are no guarantees in life. Anything can happen to anyone as per the will of God or as a result of our behaviour, both wise and foolish.*

Management Moral 2: *Questioning and doubting God may have its own spin-offs and give you the airs of a philosopher and deep thinker. But this could bring you crashing down from the topmost position.*

■ ■ ■

62. Creator and Critics

Problem

Emperor Akbar was known for his generosity, good nature and love for the arts. He patronised artists irrespective of their religious background.

Akbar wanted to test the artist in Birbal. One day, he asked Birbal if he could draw a portrait of the Emperor. Modestly, Birbal agreed and drew a reasonably good portrait of Akbar.

Akbar called a few ministers and asked them to review the portrait. The first one saw the picture from various angles and different distances. He took the artist's brush and put a dot at a particular spot.

"Hey, this does not look like the Emperor!" he said.

Another followed suit. He looked at it up and down and majestically put another dot. "Oh, this spot certainly is the one not resembling the Emperor," he declared with authority.

A few other ministers were also waiting for an opportunity to pull Birbal's leg. This was a golden opportunity for each of them. They all put dots here and there.

Birbal's Solution

Emperor Akbar said: "Birbal, how come there are so many dots these people have put on it? But the whole picture looks like me, no doubt!"

"Yes, Your Majesty! I have done a reasonable job. Let me see if these persons can draw a neat one without these blemishes, or at least correct the spot they marked. Kindly call them to do this job," Birbal requested.

When the ministers heard this, they began excusing themselves. "Oh no! The picture was good anyway, but I meant that it could be improved."

"I lost touch with the brush long ago," said another.

Each one had some excuse or the other and withdrew from the offer in utter embarrassment.

Management Moral: *Criticism comes easy. Creativity is difficult but worth the effort and much more satisfying. When the boss asks for your opinion, it is time to be serious – and not the time to pull anyone's leg, however tempting the opportunity. If you give in to insincere fault-finding, it could be a source of acute embarrassment or even have worse consequences.*

■ ■ ■

63. The Widow's Savings

Problem

A widow decided to go on a pilgrimage and visited a sadhu to leave her savings for safekeeping with him.

He told her: "Woman, I don't concern myself with money and soil my mind thinking about it. If you wish, bury your savings somewhere in my hut and when you are back, remove it from there."

She did so and proceeded on her pilgrimage. On her return, she went to the sadhu and asked for her savings.

He said: "What savings? I know nothing about your savings. I don't concern myself with money."

She said: "But you told me to bury it in your hut and go on my pilgrimage."

The sadhu said: "If you did, look for it and take it away. But don't talk to me about money."

She dug up the place where she had buried her savings but it had vanished. Disheartened, she went to seek Birbal's help and told him the whole story.

Birbal's Solution

He thought a while and instructed her to follow him to the sadhu's hut and hide behind a tree. When he prostrated before the sadhu for the second time, she should come into the hut.

The next day, carrying a jewellery box, Birbal went to see the sadhu.

Birbal prostrated before the sadhu in his hut and said: "Holy man, I am going to a far-off town and crave your blessings."

Sadhu: "You have my blessings, son."

Birbal: "I have something else to ask you, although I shouldn't bother a holy man with worldly things."

Sadhu: "Tell me, my son. May be I can help you."

Birbal: "I feel ashamed to tell you but since you are so kind, I will tell you. Please forgive me."

Sadhu: "What is it my son?"

Birbal: "I have this chest of precious stones which I have to keep safely before I go away. I am at a loss about where to keep it."

Sadhu: "I don't concern myself with money and wealth, but you can bury it in my hut and take it away when you return."

Birbal: "I am so thankful to you, Holy One, may God bless you." And he prostrated before the sadhu a second time.

153

The widow took her cue and came into the hut. 'Now this woman is going to create trouble. I had better return her miserable savings or I'll lose this man's jewels,' thought the sadhu.

He told her: "Woman, haven't you found your savings? Why don't you look in that corner?"

The widow dug up the place and found her meagre savings. Just then a messenger came in with news for Birbal. "Sir, you don't have to go on your trip. The man you were going to meet is here."

Birbal thanked the sadhu for his kindness and said he was grateful to God he did not have to trouble the sadhu as he had feared. The oversmart sadhu was left without the widow's savings or Birbal's 'jewels'!

Management Moral: *Greed is more common than we think. Watch out for it in the unlikeliest people. Refrain from playing into the hands of unscrupulous people by blindly trusting them. Once in their net, it may be difficult to extricate yourself — in personal life you may be wiped clean of your savings and in corporate life you may end up footing the bill when the person you have trusted embezzles company funds.*

■ ■ ■

64. The Holy Parrot

Problem

Emperor Akbar was once presented with a beautiful parrot. He grew so fond of the bird that he hired an attendant just to take care of the parrot!

He told the attendant: "Take good care of the parrot. If I hear anyone give me bad news about the parrot, I shall have the person beheaded."

One day the parrot, having aged, died. Remembering the Emperor's threat, the attendant ran to Birbal for help.

"Sir, please help me. The Emperor's parrot has died. If I tell His Majesty, he will have me beheaded."

Birbal told the attendant not to worry and went to the Emperor.

Birbal's Solution

"Your Majesty, your parrot has turned holy. It has taken to meditating."

"What rubbish are you talking, Birbal! You must be joking. Even you can't get a bird to meditate."

"Your Majesty, the parrot has closed its eyes and turned them skywards."

The Emperor went to see the bird and was furious. "Birbal, can't you make out this bird is dead?"

"I can. But if I were to tell you so, you would have beheaded me."

"Well, you have saved yet another head. I am grateful to you," smiled the Emperor.

Management Moral: *Break bad news gently even if its recipient doesn't have the power to behead you. Whatever the unpleasant reaction that results from the news, it will have to be faced by you. At times, it could be the shock that may be difficult for the recipient to overcome and make it difficult for you to console the person.*

■ ■ ■

65. Taking 'No' for an Answer

Problem

An ambitious courtier planned to have his son appointed treasurer in Akbar's Court. He began lobbying for him in the Court, but he knew Birbal would be against the appointment, since his son was untrustworthy.

One day, when Birbal was late for the Durbar, he asked Akbar: "Don't you think Birbal is taking the Court for granted? He should be put in his place."

Akbar: "What do you have in mind?"

Courtier: "I suggest you deny all his requests for a start."

Akbar: "All right."

Birbal's Solution

When Birbal arrived, Akbar asked him: "Birbal, why are you late today?"

Birbal: "My wife was indisposed, Your Majesty. Please forgive me."

Akbar upbraided him: "I refuse to forgive you."

Birbal: "Shall we proceed to discuss matters of the state, then?"

Akbar: "No, we shall not!"

Birbal: "In that case, perhaps you will allow me to go home."

Akbar: "No, you cannot go home."

Birbal understood something was amiss and, from the courtier's suppressed grin, knew who was responsible.

So Birbal said: "I have a last request. I request you to appoint that courtier's son your treasurer."

"No, I shall not appoint him treasurer," Akbar shot back, much to the courtier's discomfiture.

Management Moral: *Learn to turn people's negative responses into positive results.*

■ ■ ■

66. The Hen or the Egg?

Problem

At the end of Akbar's Durbar, a pandit came to the Court and said he wanted to question him. Akbar was tired and told Birbal: "Please answer the pandit's questions fast. I want to end this Durbar."

The pandit said: "I'll give you a choice. You can either answer one difficult question or a hundred easy ones."

Birbal saw Akbar would have no patience to sit through a hundred questions and opted for one difficult one.

Pandit: "Which came first, the hen or the egg."

Birbal's Solution

Birbal: "The hen, of course!"

Pandit: "How can you be so sure?"

Birbal: "I am afraid that is your second question. I agreed to answer only one!"

Management Moral: *If you want to trap somebody, ensure you close all the exit routes but don't get trapped yourself! Or else you may become an unexpected victim.*

■ ■ ■

67. Parting of Friends

Problem

Once Birbal was away on some expedition when Akbar confided to his courtiers that he was disappointed with his 16-year-old son, Prince Salim, who had a wayward friend, Yusuf, and had now adopted his friend's ways.

The courtiers offered various suggestions to Akbar, such as sending Yusuf away, telling Prince Salim what Akbar thought of Yusuf, etc. all of which Akbar rejected.

When Birbal returned, Akbar put the same problem to him.

Birbal's Solution

Birbal: "Give me two days, Your Majesty."

The next day, Birbal went to Yusuf and ensuring that Prince Salim saw them, he whispered in Yusuf's ear: "Yusuf, just one seed in every mango."

And then Birbal spoke aloud: "Don't disclose this to anyone." He then walked away.

Before long, Prince Salim approached his friend and asked: "Yusuf, what did Birbal whisper in your ear?"

"Nothing," said Yusuf.

"Yes, he did. I saw him."

"Some nonsense I couldn't understand."

"If you don't tell me, I will never speak to you again."

"Since you insist, I will tell you. He simply said, 'Just one seed in every mango'."

"I don't believe this! And I don't consider you my friend any more."

"If you don't believe me, I won't consider you my friend either." The friends walked away from each other in disgust and never spoke to each other again.

Management Moral: *It is easier to sow discord even among friends than to make people believe the truth. And it is extremely difficult to mend fences and bring together two estranged people. If we only remember this fact, we can try and avoid such situations in any work set-up.*

■ ■ ■

68. Kings and the Moon

Problem

Akbar once sent Birbal on a mission to Kabul. There he was suspected of being a spy and hauled before the local king.

King: "Who are you and what are you doing in my kingdom."

Birbal: "I am just a traveller from India."

King: "If you are such a great traveller, tell me, what do you think of my rule?"

Birbal: "You are like the full moon, no king can compare with you in power and glory."

The King was pleased with the reply, but asked: "What about your King?"

Birbal: "He is like the new moon. Nothing much to boast of."

The King was so pleased that he rewarded Birbal with a bag of gold coins.

On his return, Akbar's courtiers had already heard of Birbal's exchange with the King in Kabul and reported it to the Emperor.

Birbal's Solution

Akbar: "So, Birbal, I hear you were received by the King in Kabul?"

Birbal: "Yes, Your Majesty. He did ask me about you."

Akbar: "I hear you compared him to the full moon and me to the new moon."

Birbal: "That is true, Your Majesty."

Akbar: "How dare you insult your Emperor!"

Birbal: "I was praising you, Your Majesty. The crescent is destined for greater prosperity and increase in glory. Both the Hindus and the Muslims venerate the moon on the second day. Whereas the full moon is destined to decline in power and glory."

Akbar: "I knew I could trust you as a loyal aide."

Management Moral: *Word your messages tactfully so that the recipient gets the encomiums he is looking for without anyone else being denigrated. It takes a master to avoid telling white lies even when the whole truth cannot be told: he opts for the implied truth. Diplomacy is an art — learn it, master it, if you want to rise and hold on to the top. It is as important as fuel in your vehicle.*

■ ■ ■

69. Uses of Waste

Problem

An important traveller visiting his Court had gifted Akbar a precious vase.

Akbar: "Oh, it is chipped. Don't show me anything broken, crushed or rotten."

Birbal, who saw distress in the eyes of the visitor: "Why Your Majesty?"

Akbar: "I am surprised you ask me about such things which are of no use to anybody much less to an Emperor."

Birbal: "Not always, Your Majesty."

Akbar: "Prove it to me."

Birbal's Solution

Birbal: "From crushed sugarcane we get juice, out of which we get sugar and all kinds of delicious sweets fit for divine offering. From the broken cotton pod we get the cotton string, which is spun and woven into clothes fit for an emperor. And rotten rags, jute and other waste are used to produce paper for the Koran and our Puranas."

The Emperor agreed and apologised to the visitor for his crudeness.

Management Moral 1: *Creativity consists in finding new uses for previously unusable items.*

Management Moral 2: *Even as an important person you cannot afford to look a gift horse in the mouth. The moment you do so, you cease to be as important because you stooped so low as to be crude. Moreover, as long as the gifted horse makes a good mount its teeth don't matter.*

■ ■ ■

70. Gold Under the Pear Tree

Problem

Although an able man, the royal gardener was a miser. He would save most of his earnings, but refused to disclose the safekeeping place to anyone. One day he found all his gold missing and ran to Birbal for help.

Birbal: "Where did you hide the gold?"

Gardener: "Under the pear tree in the garden. I spend most of my day there and I thought it would be safer there."

Birbal: "Did anyone see you burying it there?

Gardener: "No, I am very careful."

Birbal's Solution

Birbal gave the matter some thought and the next day invited all the city's vaids to the Court.

There, he asked them: "Does the pear tree have any medicinal value?"

One replied: "The fruit has, but not the leaves or the flower."

But one vaid said: "The root has an important application. The other day I cured a patient suffering from jaundice with it."

Birbal: "Who is your patient?"

Vaid: "A local merchant, Hassan."

Birbal went to meet Hassan and asked him, "Who got you the root of the pear tree for your jaundice?"

Hassan: "My servant."

Birbal: "Call him here."

When the servant appeared, Birbal threatened to have him hanged if he did not return the gold. The servant readily confessed and returned the booty.

Management Moral 1: *It is easier to lose money through carelessness than to earn it or recover it when lost. As our police force cannot be compared with Birbal, it's better to be safe than sorry!*

Management Moral 2: *The most well-guarded treasure can be lost if stacked in a place accessible to the staff and a secret can be divulged even if confided to a best friend or a 'trustworthy' colleague.*

■ ■ ■

71. The Master and the Servant

Problem

Two men came to Akbar's Court, each complaining about the other. Each claimed the other was his servant who had robbed him years ago and now pretended to be the master!

Akbar asked Birbal to solve the case.

Birbal's Solution

Birbal ordered both to lie on the floor with their faces down and said: "I will now meditate. At the end of my meditation I shall know who is telling the truth and the impostor will be beheaded."

Birbal ordered the executioner to stand by and began meditating. After a few minutes, he opened his eyes. He stood behind the two men and told the executioner, "That is the impostor. Behead him."

At this, one of the men stood up and cried: "Have mercy on me. Spare my life." He was caught and punished accordingly.

Management Moral: *Guilt is the most reliable witness if it can be aroused. And there is nothing better than fear to arouse guilt. If misconduct goes unpunished, there is a tendency for the offender to take his behaviour for granted. Only the threat of losing his job may bring repentance and an apology.*

■ ■ ■

72. The Mango Tree

Problem

Huzur and Shamu came to Birbal seeking justice. Both claimed to own a mango tree since childhood, which the other wanted to usurp. After questioning them to no avail, Birbal sent both home and asked them to return the next day.

Birbal's Solution

Meanwhile, Birbal asked one of the Court attendants to sound an alarm for the two men that thieves were stealing mangoes from their tree. He would then report their reaction to Birbal.

Later, the attendant returned to say that Huzur had said he was busy with some urgent work and would see to the matter later. Shamu had rushed to the mango tree immediately to chase away the thieves.

When the two men returned the next day, Birbal told them: "Since neither of you admits that you are not the real owner, I have no option but to cut down the mango tree and divide the wood among both of you."

Huzur agreed to the decision, but Shamu said, "I have tended that tree since childhood. I don't mind losing the tree if I have to, but I can't bear to see it cut down."

Birbal could see Shamu was the real owner. He ordered Huzur to be whipped for his lies.

Management Moral: *Love cannot be easily feigned and when real love and affection is evident we can be sure that these emotions cannot lie. On the other hand, the pretence of liking your job or of being a sincere worker and exhibiting fake loyalty contrasts so sharply with the real thing that it is not difficult to know where your real loyalty lies.*

■ ■ ■

73. The Man Who Brought Bad Luck

Problem

A servant in Akbar's household had the reputation of bringing ill luck to whoever met him face to face first thing in the morning. One day, Akbar saw him as soon as he got up. Thereafter, everything seemed to go wrong for Akbar.

First his grandchild was taken ill. Then an emissary came to announce a rebellion in some remote part of the kingdom. Later, Akbar had a severe stomach-ache.

Tormented by bad news, pain and hunger, Akbar attributed it all to the servant. Seeing in him a danger to everyone in Court, the Emperor ordered the servant hanged. The servant appealed to Birbal.

Birbal's Solution

Birbal went to the Emperor: "Your Majesty, I have come to prove the servant's innocence. Can I question him in your presence?"

Akbar agreed.

Birbal called the man and asked him: "Who was the first person you saw yesterday?"

Servant: "It was the Emperor."

Birbal: "Your Majesty, you saw the servant first thing in the morning yesterday and you had several complaints.

He saw you and he is now going to lose his life. Which is a bigger misfortune?"

Realising the point Birbal was trying to make, Akbar rescinded the man's death sentence and said: "You are right, I was hasty in my judgement."

Management Moral: *Fortune and misfortune derive from your own thinking rather than from external events. We have a tendency to analyse and assign a logical reason to everything that happens in our life. Whenever the reasons are not clear we end up attributing it to luck, good or bad. Hard work and systematic management of our affairs will nullify a lot of the so-called 'bad luck' and change it into 'good luck'.*

■ ■ ■

74. Unseeing Eyes

Problem

The Queen wanted to donate money to blind people in the kingdom. A survey was made and Akbar commented that it was fortunate there were so few blind people in the kingdom.

Birbal remarked: "Your Majesty, it is unfortunate that most people have eyes but still do not see."

Akbar: "You are talking nonsense! Who has eyes and yet cannot see?"

Birbal: "You will soon discover who."

Birbal's Solution

A few days later, Birbal was seen in the centre of town stringing a charpoy. He had an assistant by his side taking down notes.

Everyone came to ask Birbal what he was doing. Birbal did not reply but asked the assistant to add another name. Eventually, the news reached the Emperor who hurried to the site.

Akbar: "Birbal, what are you doing?"

Birbal to the assistant: "Add His Majesty's name, too."

Akbar: "What kind of answer is that?"

Birbal: "I told you the other day that many people who had eyes could not see. Now everyone is asking me what I am doing though I am stringing a charpoy in broad daylight!"

Management Moral: *It sometimes takes the ability of a genius to notice the obvious! The blind may see more with their intuition than a sighted man who is not content with what his eyes tell him or refuses to accept what he sees. Make sure your auditors have sound judgement and do not belong to the group that fails to perceive things despite healthy eyes.*

■ ■ ■

75. How Many Bangles...

Problem

Once Akbar asked Birbal: "Do you know how many bangles your wife wears?"

Birbal: "No, Your Majesty. I don't know."

Akbar was elated. He had caught Birbal unawares. He told Birbal: "You are not very observant, Birbal. How can you miss the number of bangles your wife wears? You see them every day."

Birbal's Solution

Birbal: "What is the importance of the bangles. You caress your beard every day. Do you know how many hairs the beard has?"

Akbar: "What a comparison! Your wife's bangles are much bigger and fewer."

Birbal: "Every day you climb the palace stairs. They are much bigger than bangles and can be easily counted. Can you tell me their number?"

Akbar was dumbstruck.

Management Moral 1: *You cannot register and retain all that you observe. You have to be selective according to your needs. Nor is it worth your time and effort to remember insignificant details about daily life. By being selective, we can remember the important things relevant to our functioning, efficiency and relationships. For instance, it is more important to remember* *conversations with your wife or boss rather than the colour of their clothes or the type of jewellery they wear.*

Management Moral 2: *If you must criticise your subordinates, do it only when required and not for the sake of putting them down as in the latter case you end up showing yourself in poor light before others.*

■ ■ ■

76. God's Names

Problem

Akbar said to Birbal: "We Muslims have Allah, Christians have Christ, Buddhists have Buddha. But you Hindus worship so many gods. Why is it so?"

Birbal: "God is one but his names are many."

Akbar: "How is that possible? How can God assume so many forms and yet be only one?"

Birbal's Solution

Birbal summoned a servant who was wearing a turban.

He pointed to it and said: "What is that?"

Servant: "A turban."

Birbal: "Untie it, roll it and tie it to your waist."

When he had done so, Birbal asked: "What is that?"

Servant: "A Kamarband."

Birbal: "Now unroll it and tie it round your waist. What is it now?"

Servant: "A dhoti."

Birbal, turning to Akbar: "You have seen how the same cloth acquires different names when performing different functions. So also water can be a cloud when in the sky; it is rain when it falls to earth; it is a river when it flows; and it is ice when it freezes. God, too, though one, is called by different names by different people."

Management Moral: *We name things according to our own perceptions. It is important to bear in mind that the name is not the thing named. Just as a map is not the territory it refers to. Sometimes it is important to look at a thing in its entirety apart from its name to give it new applications. This is as far as things go.*

As for God, whatever we may call Him or whether we recognise Him or not, it does not change God's nature and identity. It is man who gives God various forms according to his perception. As soon as we are able to accept this fact we can direct our full energy in worshipping Him – an act that can make our lives more fruitful, rather than comparing religions and questioning God's oneness.

■ ■ ■

77. Which Hand is Up?

Problem

Once Akbar told his courtiers: "I have observed that when you give someone something, the giver's hand is above the receiver's hand. Do you know of cases where it is the other way around?"

They all said: "No, that is the way it is done in every case."

But Birbal disagreed.

Birbal's Solution

Said Birbal: "When you give snuff to someone, the receiver picks it up from the giver's open palm."

Management Moral: *It is sometimes important to know the exceptions to a rule, and the mores and customs of a place. It is also necessary to know the intricate ways of all the cultures you need to deal with so that you don't commit any blunders whilst dealing with different types of people – blunders that may lead to the loss of a client and turn out to be too costly for the organisation you work in.*

■ ■ ■

78. An Unlucky Profession!

Problem

Akbar's courtiers were forever out to get at Birbal. One day one of them asked: "Birbal, what was your profession before you came to the Emperor's Court?"

Birbal: "I was a farmer. So was my father, as well as his father and grandfather. We have been farmers for generations."

Courtier: "How did they die?"

Birbal: "They all died in the field. My father, while harvesting. His father fell into a well. His father was hit by lightning as he worked."

Courtier: "Then your profession is a very unlucky profession."

Birbal's Solution

Birbal: "What is your family's profession?"

Courtier: "We have all been soldiers."

Birbal: "How did your father die?"

Courtier: "He died in the battlefield."

Birbal: "And his father?"

Courtier: "He, too, died in battle."

Birbal: "So, a soldier's profession is equally unlucky."

Pausing, Birbal added: "All of His Majesty's ancestors died in bed. According to your argument, it must be dangerous to sleep on a bed."

Management Moral: *Luck is not a matter of profession, though some professions may be more dangerous than others. Although our lifespans are sometimes linked to the type of job we do, the obvious hazards seldom take their toll — usually, even if the job is risky, the ultimate cause of death is entirely different. This does not mean that we can afford to be unmindful of the professional hazards to our health, but if we have an obsession with our job risks, we may die of worry. Even the safest job cannot guarantee us a lucky end, as death must inevitably occur, however lucky we are.*

■ ■ ■

79. The Horse's Owner

Problem

Chandra Verma, King of Tripura, had heard of Akbar and wished to meet him. So, disguised as a merchant, he made for Akbar's kingdom on horseback. On the way he found a man who was limping, headed in the same direction. King Verma asked this man, Ravi Sharma, to mount his horse and they proceeded to their destination. On arrival, Verma got down and asked Sharma to dismount as well, but the latter refused, claiming he owned the horse!

The quarrel attracted a crowd and the two were taken to Birbal for mediation.

Birbal's Solution

Birbal asked them to return the next day, while the horse was to remain with him. As soon as they left, Birbal asked the attendant, whom he had put in charge of the horse, to take the horse out and check whom it followed.

The attendant reported that the horse had followed Chandra Verma.

The next day when the two claimants to the horse appeared, they were told to take the horse from the stable. Ravi Sharma went first but could not recognise the horse amongst all the other horses in the stable and had to return empty-handed.

As soon as Chandra Verma entered the stable, the horse began to neigh and it was easy for Verma to identify it.

Thus was the horse returned to the rightful owner and the impostor duly punished.

Management Moral: *We all have our psychological traits, which can be effectively utilised by ourselves as also by others. So do some animals, particularly domesticated ones. We also learn from the story that it is advisable to be very selective when we want to be charitable. We should first make sure that the person deserves our charity or it becomes wasteful, especially because there are so many people who deserve it and not as many who are charitable.*

This applies to organisations too — when they take up a charitable social cause, it is to society's advantage if they investigate whether the cause is really worth their attention.

■ ■ ■

80. The Crafty Tailor

Problem

Once Akbar boasted he was so sharp that no one could fool him.

Birbal replied that he knew a tailor who could steal from anyone right under his nose.

Akbar challenged Birbal to prove his point.

Birbal's Solution

The tailor was hired to stitch a blouse for the Queen. He was given a muslin cloth and warned not to play any tricks since he would be searched when leaving. A guard was posted outside the room to ensure the tailor did not take anything with him.

After some time the tailor's son came to meet him. He was not allowed to do so. So from afar he called out to the tailor to come home since his wife wanted him for lunch. The tailor told his son to go away, since he had not yet finished his work.

But the son stayed put, cajoling him to come home. Irritated, the tailor shouted at his son to go away and threw his shoe at him. The boy picked up the shoe and ran away.

When the tailor finished his work, he was thoroughly searched and allowed to go.

A few days later, the Queen's maid said she saw the tailor's wife wearing a blouse of the same cloth as the

Queen's. The tailor's house was searched; the blouse was found and confiscated.

Akbar asked Birbal how the tailor had managed to smuggle out the cloth.

Birbal smiled: "Sire, he had hidden it in the shoe he threw at his son."

Management Moral 1: *There is no limit to human ingenuity when there is sufficient motivation. Provide the motivation and you may get the moon on your desk. Conversely, the lack of sufficient motivation could lead to downing the shutters of your factory.*

Management Moral 2: *Nobody, however high his position and power, is beyond the risk of being fooled. So beware!*

■ ■ ■

81. The Masked Face

Problem

Once Akbar was so annoyed with a courtier who had absented himself that he expelled him from the Court saying: "Don't ever show me your face again."

The man went to Birbal for help. Since the man had had serious problems at home, his wife and mother both being ill and his son turning into a vagabond, Birbal decided to help him.

Birbal's Solution

A few days later, Akbar was in a depressed mood and nobody could lighten it. The same day a man entered the Court wearing a mask so funny that everyone who saw it could not help laughing.

When Akbar came in and saw the whole Court overcome with mirth, he was even more upset. He demanded to know what was going on.

When the man with the funny mask was presented before him, he too could not help laughing and his mood was lightened.

Akbar told the man: "Take off your mask and I shall reward you handsomely."

The masked man said: "Your Majesty, I can't take it off. I am the courtier whom you ordered not to show his face again to you. That is why I am wearing the mask!"

Immediately, Akbar understood this was Birbal's idea and lifted the injunction against the courtier.

Management Moral: *Where nothing else works, humour sometimes does. And when the boss is unreasonable with employees, the latter may be forced to resort to humorous tricks to save the day, their skins and their jobs. So when nothing works, try a touch of humour.*

■ ■ ■

82. Whatever I Like

Problem

There was a miser in Akbar's kingdom who lived in a decrepit hut and saved all his money, which amounted to a large number of gold coins.

One day his hut caught fire and was burning, while the miser moaned and groaned loudly without having the courage to go into his hut to rescue his savings.

A merchant was passing by and asked him, "Why are you crying so bitterly for your ramshackle hut, which is worthless in any case?"

Miser: "All my savings are in there."

Merchant: "How much can that be?"

Miser: "100 gold coins."

Merchant: "If I go in at the risk of my life, what will you give me?"

Miser: "A gold coin."

Merchant: "I risk my life and you will give me only one gold coin? That won't do. I'll do it only if you permit me to give you whatever I like."

The miser protested vociferously but finally agreed.

The merchant found out from the miser where exactly he had buried his treasure, rushed in, dug out the treasure and returned unharmed.

Said the merchant to the miser: "You agreed that I would give you whatever I like. I am keeping all the coins and giving you the bag in which they were wrapped."

The miser kept remonstrating loudly until some passers-by dragged the duo to Birbal.

The merchant explained to Birbal what had happened and demanded that he be allowed to keep all the miser's gold coins.

Birbal's Solution

Birbal asked the miser if the merchant's account was correct. The miser admitted it was.

Birbal: "Merchant, you agreed to give the miser whatever you liked. You like the gold coins don't you?"

Merchant: "I do, but..."

Birbal: "Since you like them, give them to that man as you had agreed to."

The merchant was thus compelled to do so.

Management Moral 1: *Choose your words with precision, or you may land into trouble. Language is meant to communicate our thoughts effectively. But if we talk so much and yet do not communicate with precision, all our talk is a waste of time and breath.*

Management Moral 2: *Those who frame rules and regulations should remember that unfair laws and unjust demands provoke those who are forced to comply to seek recourse in loopholes to evade the injustice. For example, there would be no black money if taxes were not too high; no strikes if employers were always fair... and the world might have been a different and better place to live in, though not totally devoid of cheaters!*

■ ■ ■

83. The Dog's Chapatti

Problem

Once when Akbar and Birbal were taking a walk, Akbar saw a dog eating a stale chapatti and said to Birbal: "Look at that dog. It is eating Kali."

Birbal: "Your Majesty, it is Niyamat for it."

Akbar: "How dare you talk like that? You know my mother's name is Niyamat. Is the dog eating her?"

Birbal: "Your Majesty knows that my mother's name is Kali. Is the dog eating her?"

Akbar: "Who was talking of your mother? I only said the dog was eating Kali, that is, black food."

Birbal's Solution

Birbal: "And I was saying that it was Niyamat, that is proper for it."

Akbar had to agree.

Management Moral: *No purpose is served by casting aspersions on people, even jokingly. Or in taking such remarks personally or seriously. It is better to maintain peace and harmony at all times with your colleagues and co-workers. But there is nothing like politely showing such a joker that the joke is in bad taste.*

■ ■ ■

84. Twig in the Beard

Problem

Akbar once again thought of outwitting Birbal. He gave his ring to a courtier in private and asked him to keep it until he asked for it.

Later he spoke to Birbal: "Birbal, today I lost my ring. I had removed the ring while having my bath and later could not find it. One of my courtiers must have stolen it. You are renowned as an astrologer. Can you tell me who has it?"

Birbal's Solution

Birbal: "Where did you keep it while having bath?"
Akbar: "On that cupboard."

Birbal went to the cupboard and lent his ear to it.

Then he said to the Emperor: "The cupboard whispered to me that the man who's got it has a twig in his beard."

The courtier who had the ring with him immediately touched his beard. Birbal thus knew he was the man and pointed him out to Akbar.

Once again, Akbar was impressed.

Management Moral: *The trickier the problem, the trickier you need to be to solve it. You need to learn about people's behaviour patterns to be able to do so. With a knack for psychology and a little practice and time to investigate, you can master the art of catching culprits who play mischief in your office or even find out if your boss is as mischievous as Akbar.*

■ ■ ■

85. Darkness Under a Lamp

Problem

Akbar and Birbal were one day watching the sunrise when they heard some noise nearby. They went to investigate and found that a party of travellers had been robbed and the robbers had decamped.

The Emperor sent his royal guard after the robbers, but to no avail. They had vanished without a trace.

Akbar told Birbal: "What is the use of being the Emperor of India if people can be robbed with impunity under my very nose?"

Birbal's Solution

Birbal replied: "Even the most powerful lamp that illuminates an area of miles around it casts a dark shadow below it."

Akbar felt consoled.

Management Moral: *Nobody is perfect. It is wise to accept your limitations rather than hanker after the unattainable. When somebody's shortcomings or failures disturb his mental peace, a few words of comfort from those he works with feel like a soothing balm. This is one reason why colleagues need to be friends, too, or the workplace can become too drab.*

■ ■ ■

86. Akbar-Bharat

Problem

One day Akbar had the brainwave of getting Birbal to write an Akbar-Bharat to compete with the Mahabharat.

Birbal's Solution

Birbal accepted the idea and after some time brought a thick sheaf of papers to Akbar: "Your Majesty, I have almost completed the first draft of the Akbar-Bharat. Now I need to clear something with the Queen. Can I meet her?"

Akbar: "Certainly. What do you want to ask her?"

Birbal: "Draupadi in the Mahabharat had five husbands. I wanted to inquire how many husbands the Queen has."

Akbar knew how insulted the Queen would feel if asked such a question and immediately scrapped the project.

Management Moral: *Don't be overambitious. It can have unpleasant consequences. Everything in moderation is the key to a balanced and happy life. The Emperor realised that offending the Queen for the sake of an Akbar-Bharat would be to let ambition and pride distort his sense of propriety and priorities.*

Besides, certain things that we crave are worth giving up for the sake of other more important issues. You may forsake a promotion to be close to your children or your family or to take care of your aged parents perhaps.

Or you may even allow your spouse the time to start a career of her own...

■ ■ ■

87. Birbal's Shocking Choice

Problem

One day Emperor Akbar asked Birbal what he would choose if he were given a choice between justice and a gold coin.

"The gold coin," said Birbal without hesitation.

Akbar was taken aback. "You would prefer a gold coin to justice?" he asked, incredulously.

"Yes," said Birbal.

The other courtiers were amazed by Birbal's display of idiocy. For years they had been trying to discredit Birbal in the Emperor's eyes but without success and now the man had gone and done it himself! They could not believe their good fortune.

"I would have been dismayed if even the lowliest of my servants had said this," continued the Emperor. But coming from you it's... it's shocking – and sad. I did not know you were so debased!"

Birbal's Solution

"One asks for what one does not have, Your Majesty!" said Birbal, quietly. "You have seen to it that in our country justice is available to everybody. So as justice is already available to me and as I'm always short of money, I said I would choose the gold coin."

The Emperor was so pleased with Birbal's reply that he gave him not one but a thousand gold coins!

Management Moral 1: *Before condemning somebody for his action, first find out why he did it. He may have a sound reason, which you may not be aware of. In all fairness, everyone should have a chance to defend himself and his actions.*

Management Moral 2: *A faithful subordinate does not miss any opportunity to praise the boss. He knows that it is to his own advantage to acknowledge the admirable qualities in a superior. It can work wonders as it did for Birbal!*

Management Moral 3: *When faced with a question by those in authority, don't always go for what seems to be the politically correct response. In all honesty if you feel otherwise, and have sound reasons to back up your response, have the courage of conviction to go against the tide. Once the management hears your logic for the unconventional response, they will appreciate the fact that you had the courage to speak the truth and go against conventional thinking. This will help you stand out in the crowd.*

■ ■ ■

Conclusion

THE KEY TO BIRBAL'S CREATIVITY

What can we learn from Birbal? Below we provide a formula for achieving greater creativity in managing our affairs and applying it to solve our problems. The problems can be of any type imaginable: relationships, career, work-related, travel, domestic, financial or other problems, the list is endless.

The Birbal narratives will give you an idea of the variety of problems that can find a satisfactory solution.

The formula can be summarised in the form of the acronym BIRBAL, each letter standing for one step of the problem-solving process, culminating in an ideal solution.

Here is the formula:

B: Begin by short-listing the problem you want to solve, out of the many that may be confronting you. (Let us say the problem you select for solving is how to manage your time, which always seems in short supply!)

I: Investigate the causes, circumstances and all available facts, listing them out on a sheet of paper. These are the various components of your problem. Some may be more important than others. (Why is your time in short supply? Do you undertake too many tasks? Are there too many interruptions? Are you a perfectionist who tinkers with a task again and again, looking for an ideal finish? Are you a procrastinator, never doing today what can be put off till tomorrow?)

R: **Relate** these components of your problem to one or more of the Birbal stories, checking for similarities and their applicability to your problem. They are not likely to fit like a glove, but may help generate ideas of your own, which you can then apply to your own problem. Read the *Management Moral* at the end of each Birbal narrative and check whether it applies to your problem. (Birbal got his wisdom from fools, learning from their mistakes. How do others waste their time? Can you learn from their mistakes? It is sometimes easier to see shortcomings in others than in yourself!)

B: **Balance** and weigh the various options available to you. Here are some option-generators you can use to come up with possible solutions:

1) Can you make one of the components of your problem bigger than the others? What does the problem look like now?

2) Can you make another component smaller and check the result?

3) Can you combine two or more of them into a single component? Will that change the nature of your problem?

Just list out the possible solutions, however outlandish they may appear at first. Don't be critical at this stage. Look for unexpected angles as Birbal used to.

When you have done this, list the solutions you think are most likely to succeed. If necessary, modify them to suit your needs. Select the solution that appears the most appealing to you. (Maybe you can combine two of your activities to reduce expenditure of time. Do your planning or some other work in the train or bus on your way to work. Instead of allotting an hour to jogging, walk briskly at least part of the way to the office. What would happen if you dropped some of your activities or delegated them to someone else in the family or workplace?)

A: Apply the solution to your problem and check the results. Does it have any unfavourable side effects? Until you apply it, you will not know. (Perhaps some activity is not being accomplished adequately. You may have to either delegate it to someone else or drop some other activity.)

L: Link the other short-listed solutions as well to your problem. Do any of them fit it better than the one you selected first? Usually the first solution is not the best solution. Select your final solution. (Perhaps you did end up saving a lot of time. That doesn't mean you can't save even more time. Try other options at different times till you feel you can no longer improve on the outcome.)

This exercise should enable you to refine and fine-tune the best solution.

Applying the BIRBAL formula should enable you to find more creative and effective solutions to your problems.

■ ■ ■

How to
Motivate Others

to turn them into super performers

—*Kurt Hanks*

A Manager's Guide for productive management

If you are asked to lead a group or assigned to manage the affairs of an office, you will probably require some tools to succeed. The tool is motivation. Without motivation there is no success. No learning. No action. And, most important of all, without motivation there are no results. This book gives a modern and more effective approach to this age old problem of lack of motivation. Each page is filled with new ideas, concepts, methods and approach. However, this book is only a tool box—the real solution comes when you effectively match and apply the ideas prescribed to the situation.

The book focuses on:
❖ The most workable formula for winning people to your way.
❖ How to move key people from where they are to where you want them to be.
❖ How to raise other's enthusiasm for your projects.
❖ What common little quirk causes more problems with other than any other and how you can avoid it.
❖ What you must see in others, that most people don't see, before you can get them to change.
❖ Secrets for dealing with stubborn people.
❖ How to make others take interest in your ideas.
❖ What everybody wants that you have.
❖ How to stop others from manipulating you.
❖ How to criticize without being resented.
❖ How to give orders that are followed effectively.
❖ How to get others to like you.
❖ How to get the ear of the key people in your organisation.

Big Size • Pages: 128
Price: Rs. 96/- • Postage: Rs. 15/-

Secrets of Leadership

Insights from the Panchatantra

—*Luis S.R. Vas*
Anita S.R. Vas

The Panchatantra is a work relevant for all times whether it is used in a Management Workshop or as a general guide to daily living. Leadership is involved in both. Through a jungle of speaking animals, a sage, Vishnu Sharma, created a storehouse of wisdom in the form of short stories for children as well as adults. These stories, written some 2,000 years ago, came to be known as Panchatantra. The influence of Vishnu Sharma's stories has been vast. By the 3rd and 4th centuries, they had already been translated into Syriac and Arabic from the original Sanskrit version. The Panchatantra has been translated into 50 different languages in some 200 different versions.

In this collection, the authors have tried to show what bearing these fables have on our leadership skills. They have highlighted some of the morals embedded in the fables themselves as well as provided modern insights at the end of each story. They have also occasionally provided relevant observations. Readers are encouraged to draw their own insights from these classic tales of wisdom.

In the conclusion, the authors have stated the five leadership secrets of the Panchatantra as revealed in the five *tantras* and combined them with a typical modern management plan designed to bring the readers' newly-learnt leadership skills to fruition.

Demy Size • Pages: 136
Price: Rs. 96/- • Postage: Rs. 15/-

Sure Success in Interviews

—Jayant Neogy

The most comprehensive one-source guide for succeeding in interviews.

This book's contents are far richer and deeper than other books on the subject. No contemporary book in the Indian market covers topics such as SWOT analysis, portfolio preparation, wardrobe tips, body language and interview preparation techniques that use question-and-answer sessions with analysis of top answers.

An exhaustive data bank of frequently asked questions and model answers ensures you hold an advantage over other candidates. Finally, there's a bonus section containing tips on good résumé writing practices.

Sure Success in Interviews is a truly comprehensive, one-source guide that will turn you into a professional performer at any interview.

This book enables you to:

• How to write a winning résumé • Practical hints to overcome nervousness & boost confidence • SWOT (Strengths, Weaknesses, Opportunities & Threats) analysis • Portfolio preparation • Tips on wardrobe & self-grooming • Understanding body language • Interview preparation techniques through Q&A sessions • The art of successful follow-up.

Demy Size • Pages: 156
Price: Rs. 96/- • Postage: Rs. 15/-

Skills for Excellence

— Luis S.R. Vas

How do you achieve excellence in a world of growing complexity and rapid technological change? The first step is a thirst for excellence. This is the motivation to achieve quality in whatever you do. Around the world numerous consultants have combined insights from behavioural sciences to train people in achieving excellence in various realms. But excellence requires skills in various areas.

In **Skills for Excellence** the author has brought together within one volume most of the ideas and practices which are being taught in enterprises around the world. The book starts with achievement motivation and shows how, as research has proved, this skill can be cultivated and developed. The other skills presented in this book are innovativeness drawn from the ideas of Peter Drucker and others; thinking skills from the concepts developed by Edward de Bono; a problem-solving technique devised by Rudolf Flesch; creativity as taught by Robert Fritz.

There are also time management, learning ability, communication skills and your retention powers. An equally basic but often neglected skill is the ability to maintain your health and fitness. All these skills are covered at length adapting ideas from masters in their respective fields.

Demy Size • Pages: 176
Price: Rs. 120/- Postage: Rs. 15/-

SUCCESS SECRETS
A Common Sense Guide to Life Long Achievement

—Merrill Douglass

This is the success secrets seminar you've been looking for!

Outstanding success is now within your reach — the keys to achieving it are in your hands! *Success Secrets* gives you *all* the powerful, life-changing guidance and direction you need to reach your full potential in your personal and professional life.

These dynamic success secrets won't just help you get to the top of your field, they'll enable you to get more of everything you want — on the job, in your relationships, and even in your leisure time. You'll master dozens of expert techniques for:

❖ managing your time
❖ setting reachable goals
❖ presenting a professional image
❖ getting ahead in your career
❖ leading effectively
   and much more!

Internationally-known speaker and time-management seminar leader, Dr. Merrill Douglass, delivers your keys to success in concise mini-chapters that are easy to read even on your busiest days! You'll turn to them again and again for quick reference, challenging direction, and uplifting encouragement.

A world-class course in achievement, this collection of super-motivating secrets will help you reach and exceed your loftiest dreams! You don't need a seminar on success. All you really need is *Success Secrets*.

Demy Size • Pages: 256
Price: Rs. 120/- • Postage: Rs. 15/-

Build Self-confidence

—*Alankrita*

Practical guidelines to personal and professional success

Life is never a bed of roses. However, if we know how to negotiate our way between the thorns and hurdles of life, the roses of success will be ours for selective picking. The greatest asset in the quest for success and happiness is our measure of self-confidence. More than half of all life's battles are won or lost in the mind. Therefore, a person needs to saturate his or her mind with positive thoughts at all times. Our mind will then play host to many big ideas. Converting these big ideas into practical goals and long-term success calls for dollops of vision, hard work and perseverance.

This book shows you how to shake off all the sloth and lethargy and get cracking right away on your tasks and goals in life. The book is liberally sprinkled with myriad stories, anecdotes and events that inspire us to follow in the footsteps of those who achieved greatness. It teaches you how to overcome old habits and encumbrances on your journey to the highest peaks and how to mould your circumstances, rather than be moulded by them. And once you learn to face life head-on with loads of self-assurance and self-confidence, success and well-being will be yours for the asking.

Demy Size • Pages: 160
Price: Rs. 80/- • Postage: Rs. 15/-

Create your own Success Story & Live Life King-Size

—*Bindu S. Nair*

Through anecdotes, jokes and sayings,
the book guides you about:
- *Creating your own opportunities*
- *The importance of planning and persistence*
- *Timely action and living in the moment*
- *The power of dreams, vision and positive thinking*

Throughout life, we strive for personal and professional success. While many do succeed, others may still be seeking to fulfil their goals. This book gives broad guidelines to tap the boundless opportunities that exist all around us, which many leave untapped.

However, success is not everything in life. This book is based on the idea that, while success is important, one should also know how to be a wonderful person and enjoy one's success. In the race for success, we should not forget to enjoy every moment of life.

The first part of the book presents tips and practical advice about how you can create your own success story. The second part talks about how you can transform yourself into a better human being. And the third part deals with how to enjoy every moment of your existence, enjoy your success and spread positive energy all around you. Read, understood and imbibed thoroughly, this book can be the catalyst that could transform your life forever.

Demy Size • Pages: 112
Price: Rs. 96/- • Postage: Rs. 15/-